T0064498

ROLLING IN SPECIAL DIRT

Walt Babich

authorHOUSE®

AuthorHouse™
1663 Liberty Drive
Bloomington, IN 47403
www.authorhouse.com
Phone: 1 (800) 839-8640

© *2015 Walt Babich. All rights reserved.*

No part of this book may be reproduced, stored in a retrieval system, or transmitted by any means without the written permission of the author.

Published by AuthorHouse   09/30/2015

ISBN: 978-1-5049-2097-1 (sc)
ISBN: 978-1-5049-2096-4 (e)

Library of Congress Control Number: 2015910759

Print information available on the last page.

Any people depicted in stock imagery provided by Thinkstock are models, and such images are being used for illustrative purposes only. Certain stock imagery © *Thinkstock.*

This book is printed on acid-free paper.

Because of the dynamic nature of the Internet, any web addresses or links contained in this book may have changed since publication and may no longer be valid. The views expressed in this work are solely those of the author and do not necessarily reflect the views of the publisher, and the publisher hereby disclaims any responsibility for them.

"*H*ANNAH SLUMBERS 'NEATH THE SWEET *gum tree...*" were the words of the Stephen Ray Stickle song going through Eggplant Charlie's mind as he hung pieces of jute twine from a rickety framework in his cucumber patch. Things were going quite well it seemed. Everything was in a sort of balance. The early summer/late spring sweetness of this corner of the world manifested itself in the aroma of honeysuckle, and aside from the old minstrel song playing in his head, the only detectable sounds were those of a redwing blackbird and...

...the clucking, chucking, clicking noise from a damned squirrel. Eggplant Charlie detested squirrels ever since they ruined his experimental patch of sweet corn the previous year. He had been proud of that patch. It was knee high long before the fourth of July, and the ears were filling out nicely when, looking out from his dinner table, he spied two jolly frolicking squirrels climbing the stalks and joyfully breaking them for seemingly no reason at all.

Cauliflower was in the mint patch selecting sprigs for home-brewed tea. She was happy, as usual, and as usual, was immune to Eggplant Charlie's contagious grouchiness.

Eggplant Charlie picked up a stone as the squirrel neared his patch of jalapenos. He had resolved to teach this squirrel a lesson. He waited until Cauliflower had her back turned before he let the stone fly. It wouldn't do to have her see him actually peg the stone, but if all she would see would be the injured squirrel or the squirrel running away, then she would probably not be upset because she was usually bad at making cause and effect connections unless she could plainly see both cause and effect occurring simultaneously.

He let fly and hit the squirrel squarely on the head. *Bull's-eye!*

Damn. The elation went away almost instantly when he saw that he had killed it. It was a good shot. Powerful. Accurate. It turned the squirrel's lights right off. Thing was, Eggplant Charlie was a grouch, but he mainly just wanted to be left alone. He didn't want to hurt anybody, much less kill anybody, but there was the body—dead as a doornail. *Now where did that expression come from? Dickens? Mr. McGoo's Christmas Carol?* In Eggplant Charlie's opinion, Mr. McGoo had a fine way of presenting the classics. Mr. McGoo's version of *Moby Dick* was about as close to reading *Moby Dick* as Eggplant Charlie would ever get. *Aw well, poor squirrel. Glad Cauliflower didn't see that.*

Cauliflower was busy gathering raspberries. She was singing another Stephen Ray Stickle song and getting the words all wrong.

"Massa is gone; he's in the ground

But he'll be coming back around

Maybe this time as a cow."

Eggplant Charlie barely remembered the original words, but he knew they definitely had nothing to do with reincarnation.

Anyway, Cauliflower was sweet, and she could sing. Her voice added harmony to the symphony of redwing blackbird chirps, cicada clicks and two-stroke engines. This kind of symphony fulfilled any need Eggplant Charlie may have had for music. He hadn't deliberately listened to the radio in years.

Everything was fine. Everything fit, including the beans, the raspberries, the cucumbers, the okra, the tomatoes, the muscatine grapes, and, of course, the eggplants for which he was famous. Everything was coming up roses, including the roses.

There was a place for everything and everything was in its place. The lumber from the barn he had bought and torn down was now neatly stacked, the nails having been pulled and the unsalvageable separated from the salvageable. Three non-running 1970 GMC pickups sat on blocks so that his one running version would not soon want for parts. The cellar was full of canned vegetables from last year. The freezer was full of fish he had caught and road-killed deer. Cords and cords of firewood bordered one side of his property like a stone wall. Eggplant Charlie was rich, at least by Eggplant Charlie's standards.

The only thing that didn't fit was the dead squirrel. Of what use was a dead squirrel?

Well, there was an answer. Eggplant Charlie didn't like *squirrels*, but he liked *squirrel* well enough. He wasn't a vegetarian, despite his name. He didn't hunt, but he traded vegetables with the hunters at the co-op for meat, and he occasionally dined on fresh road kill, although there were certain animals he wouldn't eat, no matter how freshly killed. He wouldn't eat any predatory or carrion-eating animal. He would pass on the possum, thank you. However, freshly killed deer or rabbit were definitely edible, as was squirrel, provided it was smothered in gravy.

He approached the dead critter. If it were stiff, he'd just toss it. He picked it up by the tail and shook it, and it was loose and limber. So far, so good. He was feeling philosophical, so he brought it close to his face so that he could apologize to it and let it know that its protein would not go to waste.

The squirrel came back to life and bit Eggplant Charlie's face again and again. Eggplant Charlie dropped the squirrel and yelled for Cauliflower. As soon as the squirrel hit the ground, he began walking, or limping around Eggplant Charlie with his head cocked to one side.

Eggplant Charlie would probably have done better if had hollered "Fire!" or even "Help!"

Calling Cauliflower by name by no means indicated to Cauliflower that an emergency was in progress. People at the co-op shouted "Cauliflower!" all the time. That didn't mean much. There was a spill somewhere, or she had put a box somewhere where people could trip over it or something. "Cauliflower!" – well, she heard it all the time. Eggplant Charlie called her by name mostly when he was feeling grouchy. He usually called her "baby" or "sweetie". Something must be wrong, she thought. If she waited long enough, maybe it would fix itself.

Eggplant Charlie was losing blood. He was in shock and feeling dizzy. To add insult to injury, the squirrel was making goofy orbits around him, limping, and with his head oddly cocked.

"Rabies! That would explain it!" thought Eggplant Charlie. *"Damn, I'm gonna have to get those shots!"*

"Come here now! I need you!" he screamed. He changed the pitch of his voice just enough to let Cauliflower know that he wasn't just angry. Something was seriously wrong.

Cauliflower could plainly see that two sentient beings were suffering in her immediate vicinity. Poor Eggplant Charlie! Poor squirrel! Who needed help the most? Eggplant Charlie's face was covered in blood, and the squirrel was limping and acting odd for a squirrel. Cauliflower kissed Eggplant Charlie to calm him down, and, in the process, she got blood all over her face and her tee shirt. Then, she scooped up the squirrel and walked toward the functioning GMC, pulling Eggplant Charlie along by the hand.

Eggplant Charlie felt that his head might explode. He was in a lot of pain, and he was pretty confused. It seemed as if Cauliflower would be in charge now, and that he would be at her mercy. He was dismayed at the fact that the squirrel would be coming along, too, and he wasn't crazy about the way that Cauliflower looked right then, kind of like a tender-hearted vampire who had just eaten. Eggplant Charlie really didn't like the fact that Cauliflower would be driving. She had never really gotten the hang of braking, and she always gave him mild whiplash when she was at the wheel. Nevertheless, Eggplant Charlie was too weak and too helpless to do much of anything but suffer.

Let's call the squirrel Sam. His name was not Sam, but there is no point in trying to come up with a translation for it or attempt a phonetic transcription. Squirrels have names, more or less, but they don't think much like we do when it comes to naming each other. There are no squirrel saints, for example, so Thomas or Peter or John won't really suffice. The closest phonetic approximation would entail using some of the International Phonetic Alphabet's representations of some sounds from the click languages of southern Africa, but even this would fall short because squirrel language involves a lot of sustained sounds and repetitions. Sam's name was pronounced by making six alveolar clicks with alternating rising and falling pitches followed by seven flat clicks in rapid succession.

Sam wasn't thinking straight. He had been clobbered by a rock and his brain had been jostled a little. If you wonder what squirrels think about, well, every squirrel is a little bit different, but they don't tend to dwell on the afterlife or make plans more than an hour, on the outside, into the future. They do think, however, and they do talk.

The talk is mostly about territory. "Hey, I was here first." They also engage in sweet talk. "Come here, you. I'm in the mood for copulation, and you are the only other squirrel around here.' Squirrels, for the most part, though, are doers, not talkers.

This is a trait that Sam --A.K.A. Six-Alveolar Clicks-With-Alternating-Rising-and-Falling- Pitches-Followed-by-Seven-Flat-Clicks-in-Rapid Succession -- and most other squirrels shared with Eggplant Charlie, who, when compared with most other humans, spoke relatively little. Eggplant Charlie liked to *do* stuff, rather than talk about it, but it was not the same stuff that Sam liked to do.

Sam liked to jump, mostly. He wasn't a flying squirrel, but the feeling he got when he was in the upper canopy of the trees in Eggplant Charlie's neighborhood, leaping from one skinny branch that could barely hold his weight to another, was like the feeling Eggplant Charlie could only dream about when he was experiencing his happiest recurring dream, the flying dream. In this dream Eggplant Charlie was not constrained by gravity, and he moved like the astronauts. Then, Cauliflower would kick him and gravity would return. For Sam, however, gravity had seemed like a minor obstacle as he jumped from branch to branch.

Eggplant Charlie was bleeding like a stuck pig inside the GMC pickup. Cauliflower was driving like Cauliflower, having never quite mastered the interplay between clutch, brake and accelerator, and getting them confused at times. To make matters worse, Cauliflower didn't know exactly where she was going. She was of two minds, torn between going to the vet to fix up the squirrel or to the emergency room to get help for Eggplant Charlie.

Cauliflower was not really a talker, but she was not really a doer, either. Cauliflower was a *be-er*, if there is such a word. Her true mission in life was to *be*. Almost everyone recognized this fact upon meeting her, and most had sense enough not to expect a lot of production from her. She had a "job" at the co-op, which wasn't really a "job" in the traditional sense because it only paid in discounts and free groceries, but it gave her a place to *be* that was outside of her and Eggplant Charlie's property boundaries, and it gave her what amounted to her social life.

Cauliflower was, by far, the most inept "worker" at the co-op, and she had some serious competition. Most go-getters are not interested in working jobs that pay no money, so the level of incompetence at the co-op was fairly high. There were always long lines at the cash register as the cashiers frequently seemed to forget that they were checking people out, and preferred to focus on conversations they were having with each other or with customers.

Cauliflower, however, was in a class of her own at the co-op. She was simply incapable of operating a cash register. She mostly shelved groceries, but she would get distracted and leave boxes in the middles of aisles or put the products in the wrong places. In short, she screwed up a lot.

From a purely profit-driven point of view, Cauliflower should have been fired. She was more of a liability than an asset, but from that perspective, nobody in the industrialized world should have children because they are nothing but a drain on their parents' assets. It is mysterious, yet somehow right, that modern folks still want children even though these kids will never help them make a living, or, in many cases, even help them out in their old age. People still have kids because kids should *be.* Cauliflower added something to the co-op that couldn't be measured in dollars and cents. She just *was.* If anyone complained about her screw-ups, someone else was usually quick to reply, "Aw, let her *be.*"

Well, almost. There was another reason for Cauliflower's job security at the co-op. Eggplant Charlie, while not exactly a celebrity, produced a celebrated product, which was, of course, eggplant. Several relatively famous chefs in Philadelphia and Baltimore mentioned his eggplant in their blogs. Feature articles in *The Sun* and *The Inquirer* occasionally mentioned it as well. The eggplant even earned a shout out on one of the "foodie" shows, during which the host/chef said, "I only use local, organic eggplant in my parmesan, and the best place around here to get it is from a local fellow called Eggplant Charlie, who supplies the Italian market and most of the Oriental groceries here in the tri-state area."

That was amazing stuff among the co-op crowd, but Eggplant Charlie was hardly a rock star. *Celebrity* is a relative term, and Eggplant Charlie was celebrated enough to guarantee Cauliflower's tenure at the co-op, but not enough to get him or her much else except customers.

Cauliflower decided that the squirrel needed help more urgently than did Eggplant Charlie. Triage was not something with which she had much experience, and, evidently, she wasn't very good at it. Eggplant Charlie had become zombie-like due to loss of blood, whereas Sam had a squirrel-sized headache, but his recuperative process, like his metabolism, was much speedier than Eggplant Charlie's.

Eggplant Charlie no longer much cared about anything. He felt he was dying in a 1970 GMC pickup, accompanied by his old lady, who had blood all over her face and tee-shirt from trying to kiss his troubles away, and by the squirrel that had mauled his face. He was resigned to the likelihood that he was going to die because Cauliflower figured the squirrel needed help more than he did. *"Okay then,"* he thought. *"No Problem."*

The GMC came to a halt in front of the State Line Veterinary Associates. Cauliflower opened the door to get Sam, but Sam took the opportunity to leap out of the truck and run up a tree. Cauliflower had no idea what to do, so she shouted for help. "Help me! Get that squirrel!" she hollered.

Now, all this took place after the advent of cellphones, YouTube and viral videos, and poor Cauliflower was about to receive her fifteen minutes of fame.

Certain aspects of human nature seemed to have changed in a relatively short time. One of these might be the way in which people react to a fellow human who is in what appears to be life threatening distress. In the 1960s, a woman in New York City was brutally murdered within sight and earshot of an entire apartment building, and nobody called the police. In the 1990s, a passerby with a camcorder filmed an incident of police brutality in Los Angeles and sent it to a T.V. station. The video provoked enough outrage to cause a riot.

It is relatively easy to criticize the behavior, if inaction can be called behavior, of the New York apartment dwellers, but what about the behavior of the camcorder operator? Obviously he or she could not have called the police because the police were the villains in that case. It would also be unrealistic to expect the camcorder operator to have physically intervened, since the only reasonable outcome, had such a plan been followed, would have been a smashed camcorder and a tased and dazed camera person with a lot of tissue damage. Anyway, filming is action, it's not inaction, but what about sending the film to the media? It was probably the right thing to do, but it caused a lot of people a lot of pain.

There is no excuse for the behavior of those who encountered the drama in front of the veterinarian's office. It is easy enough to dial the emergency number 9-11 these days, and it is ridiculously easy when a person already has a smart phone handy. However, none of the first three witnesses even considered calling the 9-11 dispatcher. They focused on what they saw as a comical scene, and on their potential to be cyberspace cinematographers. They decided to film the episode with their phones and post the videos on the internet.

One of the videos showed a blood-soaked lady screaming, "Get that squirrel! The squirrel needs help!" Then, the camera panned to the seat of the GMC, in which

Eggplant Charlie, also soaked in blood, had passed out. It was an intriguing piece of film, but, aside from the ethical problems involved in taking pictures instead of helping out, there remains a question of genre. Was it journalism? Was it art? Was it just sensationalist garbage?

Oddly enough, it was identified as art by an art critic writing for *The New York Times.* The critic argued that it was edgy and disturbing, and it made people think. Those seemed to be his criteria for placing the video in the category of *art.* The critic also placed it in the sub-category of *found* art, art similar in some ways to the sculpture *Fountain* by Marcel Duchamp. *Fountain* was a urinal that Duchamp found and tried to display at an art show in 1917. Whereas some people thought of *Fountain* as the death of art, the *New York Times* critic thought it was the beginning of true art, as defined by the aforementioned criteria. The critic saw the video of Cauliflower and Eggplant Charlie as the rebirth of true art. Perhaps this was evidence that the spirit of Duchamp still walked the Earth, having descended from a heavenly staircase in the raw.

That was the highbrow reaction. The middle and lowbrows just went to YouTube or sent each other links so that countless office workers in untold numbers of cubicles could watch films entitled:

Vampire Woman Looking for Squirrel

Or

Help the Squirrel!

These titles were translated into Spanish, Portuguese, Chinese, German, Japanese, French and Russian. Instant internet fame--who needs it?

Not Eggplant Charlie. He didn't have much use for the internet, although he had a website and sold some of his canned produce that way. He just didn't care much for being indoors and pushing buttons.

Sam had absolutely no use for the internet. No squirrel did.

Cauliflower liked e-mail and communicated with some friend on Skype, and she liked the music videos on you tube, but now what Eggplant Charlie called "the son-of-a-bitch internet" was about to screw Cauliflower but good.

Eggplant Charlie had gone into another realm by the time the first responders came onto the scene. Those who recorded the scene for future postings did not summon the first responders. That credit goes to a passerby of African-American ethnicity.

Many years ago, the great tunesmith Stephen Ray Stickle realized that the heart and soul of America was African-American, and so the heroes and heroines in his songs were mostly black. This was no accident. Who else really understands forgiveness? Who else feels the Holy Ghost within them, telling them to do what is right? Who is statistically much more likely to help a stranger in distress than anyone else? These admirable traits are not coded in one's D.N.A., so don't expect a racist argument or one supporting the moral superiority of one group of Homo sapiens over another. There is another explanation. Nobody gets to choose the skin or situation into which they will be incarnated or reincarnated. Neither is it purely a question of karma. Maybe the owner of a slave ship is now a single mom in Detroit dealing with the poverty and the degradation that he/she set in motion in a previous life, but he/she is much more likely to be a cockroach now than a human being. On the other hand, the single mom may be a Buddha who actually volunteered to be sent back to Earth. There's just no telling. The skin and situation in which you find yourself is kind of a garden, and, just as different vegetables are cultivated in different gardens, different character traits, good and bad, can be best cultivated under different circumstances. So, yes, melons grow best in sandy soil, and good samaritanism grows best in the African-American community. However, as any county agent will tell you, the soils in which certain vegetables will grow best will also nurture certain weeds. All that being said, it was a black guy, who, upon seeing a seemingly crazed woman covered in blood and hollering about a squirrel and a man who appeared to be mortally wounded, had the wherewithal to use his cellphone to call for help rather than to obtain internet glory. By the way, the Good Samaritan was plenty drunk at the time, so maybe he wasn't a paragon of virtue, after all.

Eggplant Charlie was in another dimension. The here and now of bleeding to death in the front of a 1970 GMC pickup was oddly irrelevant. So what? He had a painful tug which drew him back to reality for a nanosecond. What about Cauliflower? Who would take care of her once he was gone? Then a feeling of peace overtook him.

He heard the words of Stephen Ray Stickle: *Let others raise their glasses; in that joy I can't partake*, and then he saw him, big as life, or small as life, because in life he appeared small.

Ah, Stephen Ray Stickle, born in Orwigsburg, Pennsylvania in 1826, the very man who wrote the soundtrack to Eggplant Charlie's life was right there in the flesh. Yes, right there. Where was there? Right next to Eggplant Charlie—big bow tie, stinky white shirt and coat, longish hair, mustache, sad, baggy Anglo-Saxon eyes. *Son of a bitch, in the flesh, big as life....*

"Massa done played his final tune, and my lady done sang her song, so fare-thee-well to both them two, I'd best be getting along," sang the songsmith.

If you could be in the presence of anyone, living or dead, real or unreal, who would you choose? For Eggplant Charlie it was the man in the fat bow tie who smelled like gin. He had no idea what to say, so he started with a banal greeting.

"So, how are you doing?" asked Eggplant Charlie, despite his assumption that this meeting was impossible.

"I'm a hundred fifty years dead sir. I'm not *doing* much at all these days."

"I'm a big fan of yours."

"A big *what* sir?"

"I enjoy your music very much."

"Thank you, sir. I've traveled quite a lot, you know, and people have been most gracious. I've been from South Carolina to Ohio, and people have always been so kind to me, and so respectful."

Eggplant Charlie had traveled much more extensively. He'd been to Europe. He'd been to Mexico and Guatemala. He had been to maybe thirty five states, but, then again, he had had access to transportation that Stephen Ray Stickle could only dream about.

Sam had never traveled more than a half mile from where he was born, and he was completely lost. He had not been immune to Cauliflower's charms. When she picked him up, his instincts should have told him to bite her the way that he had bitten Eggplant Charlie, but something inside him overrode those instincts and allowed her to scoop him up and put him in the cab of the pickup. Lord have mercy! This was no place for a squirrel, but Cauliflower's presence comforted him enough. He was aware that Eggplant Charlie was also in the truck, but he intuitively understood that Eggplant Charlie was no threat to anybody and was probably on his way out of this life.

Where that intuitive notion was coming from was another story. Squirrels don't live very long. Due to traffic accidents, urban squirrels rarely reach their third birthdays, not that birthdays are observed by squirrels. As an exurban squirrel, Sam was relatively old at four. Notions of death rarely crossed Sam's mind, even moments after witnessing it.

In all squirrel languages, there is a distinction between *squirrel* and *not-squirrel*. One day, about a month before Eggplant Charlie threw a rock at him, Sam was chasing a female squirrel, intending to woo her and get some copulating done. He followed her as she ran across the asphalt of the road that ran perpendicular to Eggplant Charlie's driveway, whereupon a car hit her. Although her tail was still twitching, in Sam's mind, the thing in the road was *not-squirrel*, not former squirrel, not dying squirrel, not sister squirrel—just *not squirrel*.

An approximation of Sam's thought process, greatly slowed down because squirrels are relatively quick, if not deep, thinkers might be, *"Avoid not-squirrel if there is no percentage in engaging not-squirrel. I must leave."*

And so Sam left the scene with no more thought about the incident. His brain saw no need to move the incident from his working memory to his long-term memory. Half an hour later, he had completely forgotten about it.

Now, Sam was in an alien environment--the truck,-- with two not-squirrels. He was still a little confused from having been brained by Eggplant Charlie's rock, but he was getting over his stupor. Cauliflower threw him --not literally of course. There was something about her that said *squirrel* or even *the mother of all squirrels*, but he began to feel as if this was a foolish misconception. Therefore, when the door to the truck opened, he bolted. He attempted to run up a tree trunk, but his equilibrium was off and he fell, which horrified Cauliflower, the mother of all squirrels. She was so concerned about the squirrel's well-being that she hollered for help, which, of course, attracted the attention of the sociopathic smart phone cinematographers.

Eggplant Charlie's conversation with Stephen Ray Stickle had taken another turn. It would seem now that two characters from a minstrel show, Mr. Bones and Mr. Interlocutor, were hovering over him in the back of an ambulance.

"How many fingers am I holding up?" asked EMT Bones.

"As many as I can see…" answered Eggplant Charlie, attempting to take his place in the line of minstrels. There was Mr. Bones (EMT), Mr. Interlocutor (EMT), and Mr. Tambo (Eggplant Charlie). Life—or death—was a merry minstrel show complete with Stephen Ray Stickle music. This was agreeable to Eggplant Charlie.

"Captain, the engines can't take it anymore. The dilithium crystals are spent and the matter-anti-matter reactors are on the fritz!" hollered Scottie, the ambulance driver.

"Fare-thee-well, Miss Annabelle, 'till I'm back in Caroline," sang the two EMTS and Eggplant Charlie in perfect harmony.

What about Miss Anabelle? Last Eggplant Charlie had seen her was…. aw, shoot! Where was Cauliflower?

Where the hell was Anabelle? This could have been fun. He had been ready to step into the light in the company of Bones, Interlocutor, Scottie, and Stickle, but now he had to stick around and get it together for Cauliflower's sake. She needed him.

"Sir, who is the president of the United States?"

They ask patients this question to determine whether or not they are all there after a traumatic experience. They don't ask the patient's name, because patients have a way of getting very agitated if they can't remember their own names.

Eggplant Charlie was stuck between realities. Should he give a straight answer, or play his part in the minstrel line? He figured that the minstrel line was probably unreal, but that Bones, Interlocutor and Scottie were real, but, in this dimension, had been transformed into two EMTs and an ambulance driver. Stickle, apparently, was real and as big as life, sitting by Eggplant Charlie in his stinky suit that he had bought in 1849, and that he had never washed. He smelled like a distillery. He was taking Eggplant Charlie's pulse and winking. That's *winking* not *blinking,* timed at intervals to let Eggplant Charlie know that he was sending a message and that he was not suffering from a nervous tic or some neurological symptom of alcoholism.

"Give me a hint," said Eggplant Charlie reasonably.

"I can't get a straight answer out of this cat. He's high on something," said Bones.

Eggplant Charlie didn't like the sound of that. He was pretty far gone, but a good chunk of his brain realized that he was going to the hospital for treatment, and his chances of getting what he needed might be seriously reduced if those in charge thought that he was drunk or stoned.

"I'm not high. I don't do drugs."

"How come your old lady did this to you?" asked Mr. Interlocutor.

"Where's Cauliflower?"

"See what I mean? He's not making any sense whatsoever."

Stickle winked and whispered, "*Starlight and sunshine will e'er light your way; moonbeams depart at the first sight of day.*"

While Eggplant Charlie was enjoying the relatively compassionate treatment afforded most ambulance passengers, Cauliflower was being treated in a completely different way.

When the police arrived on the scene, they saw what millions of YouTube fans would later see, an agitated woman, completely soaked in blood and screaming about a squirrel, while the man whom she had evidently just stabbed or bit was dying a few yards away.

They drew their weapons on Cauliflower, who screamed and tried to run away. Fortunately, nobody shot her, not with a gun at least. They tased her, sending electrified darts into her body. This, of course was horrible, but it was catnip for the internet audience, and it was described as a *coup de grace* by the *New York Times* art critic.

Cauliflower, who felt remorse whenever she slapped a mosquito, was writhing in pain because the police thought she was responsible for mauling Eggplant Charlie. The true culprit had finally managed to make it up a strange tree, but he was feeling wobbly. Nobody was looking for him. Nobody thought Cauliflower's words were anything but rants, but if they had understood the real sequence of events, they would have, indeed, been interested in catching the squirrel, and if they had succeeded in catching the squirrel, they would have tested it for rabies, which would have been disastrous for Sam as it would have involved getting his head cut off.

Cauliflower was not guilty of anything as serious as mauling Eggplant Charlie, nor was she particularly crazy, at least by an old standard. The standard works like this: people tend to be very uncomfortable in the presence of someone who is truly mentally ill. However, people wanted Cauliflower around. She had a calming effect on those in her presence rather than a disturbing one. Nevertheless, she was guilty of having a bad sense of priority as she thought Sam needed help more than Eggplant Charlie, and she was also guilty of tying her shoes in a watermelon patch.

The last line is metaphorical, of course, and it comes from a Chinese proverb: "Don't tie your shoes in a watermelon patch." If you do, people will suspect that you are stealing watermelons. The police thought that Cauliflower, being covered with blood and screaming what appeared to be nonsense, was insanely trying to kill, and perhaps eat, Eggplant Charlie, so they tased her.

Eggplant Charlie used to be convinced that every stranger in his watermelon patch was really trying to steal his watermelons. Unfortunately, he was mostly right. He would point an unloaded twenty two at the would-be thieves and holler, after which they would skedaddle, reinforcing his misanthropic point of view.

One guy wouldn't be intimidated, though. He said, "Go ahead and shoot. I don't care."

Eggplant Charlie approached him and said, "It's not loaded, anyhow, but those watermelons cost money and take time and hard work to grow, and I can't be giving them away."

"I'm not stealing. I'm just taking a shortcut."

Eggplant Charlie could have given the stranger a lecture about trespassing, and he could have told him to get off his land, but for all his grouchiness, Eggplant Charlie never kicked anybody off "his" land unless the person was clearly up to no good.

Eggplant Charlie did not come from a long line of farmers, but he was always fascinated by farming. He came of age at the time when the so-called "back-to-the-land" movement was in its death throes. Urban hippies had tried farming, discovered it was hard, and went back to the cities and found work. A handful made it, however, and these folks became Eggplant Charlie's role models. After working like a coolie at construction jobs, Eggplant Charlie finally managed to put a down payment on a fifty-acre spread in Maryland. As he was figuring out how to farm, he continued working non-farming jobs, using his skills in carpentry, welding, and painting and even doing a little unlicensed and off-the-books electrical and plumbing work. He reached a modicum of success by specializing in fresh organic vegetables, especially Asian vegetables, and by selling them at farmer's markets and ethnic grocery stores. The internet allowed him to find a mail order market for some of his goods, and the endorsements of some famous chefs, as mentioned before, enhanced his professional reputation. His farm grew to one hundred and sixty acres, which is nothing for a cash crop farm, but it was plenty for a gifted horticulturalist like Eggplant Charlie.

Nevertheless, as he was acquiring this land, he never forgot what it was like to love the land but not to own any. As a teenager, he had been threatened and chased off countless properties just because he wanted to be outside without crowds of people around him. After he had secured his own little slice of heaven, he vowed to be tolerant of "trespassers", provided they weren't harming anything.

As it turns out, the guy who wasn't stealing watermelons became one of Eggplant Charlie's few friends, for a while, anyway. Eggplant Charlie found some work for him through his old construction contacts, and as it turned out, the guy was a relatively decent folk musician and was able to get a gig in town on Friday and Saturday nights.

Eggplant Charlie would go into town to watch his newfound friend perform, and, of course, he would bring Cauliflower. The musician, who called himself Mark Metacomet, claimed to be part Wampanoag Indian and a direct descendant of King Phillip. He included a lot of traditional tunes in his set, even a Stephen Ray Stickle song or two at Eggplant Charlie's request. In addition, he always incorporated at least one original song in the act, one that was usually about a local character, preferably one in the audience, and that was the cause of the falling out between Eggplant Charlie and Mark Metacomet.

Mark Metacomet sang songs about everybody associated with the co-op—Redneck Davey, Bertha the Lesbian Roofer, Cauliflower, Eggplant Charlie—everybody. This was all in good fun, and all the subjects of the songs were able to enjoy a laugh at their own expense. One evening, however, Mark Metacomet introduced an original by saying, "I have a song here that underscores the old saw, ` You can lead a horse to water, but you can't lead a horticulture.'" He went on to sing, *"Eggplant Charlie likes the sporting life, but at the end of the day, he goes home to his wife."* The audience loved it but Cauliflower was not amused.

She thought that Metacomet was singing about an affair that Eggplant Charlie was having. In reality, Eggplant Charlie was completely innocent of infidelity, and being falsely accused angered him. Cauliflower finally either forgave or forgot the imagined indiscretion, but forgiveness and forgetfulness were not traits that Eggplant Charlie either exhibited or cultivated. His friendship with Mark Metacomet was over.

Sam the squirrel was in enemy territory. He was far from home. The trees were strange. The squirrel dialect spoken in this neck of the woods was incomprehensible to him. He was surrounded by *squirrel*, but they felt like *not-squirrel*. When then chattered at him, it was clear that they were saying, "Get out!" "Go home!" and "You are *not-squirrel!*"

"Do you know where you are?" It was Scottie. Kirk, Bones, and Mr. Interlocutor were also about. Eggplant Charlie couldn't see Stickle, but he could smell his gin and b.o., so he sensed his presence.

"*I'm in a hospital,*" is what Eggplant Charlie tried to say. However, it sounded more like,

"Nomenanahspell."

"Mr. Tambo?"

"Yes, Mr. Interlocutor?" responded Eggplant Charlie, eager to take his place in the minstrel line once again.

"What do you think about laissez-faire economic policy?"

"Well, if you lazy, you ain't gonna fare very well, is you, Mr. Interlocutor?"

"Who is the president of the United States?" asked a disembodied voice of authority.

Now, torn between two realities, one being answering questions in a hospital and the other being part of a minstrel show, Eggplant Charlie chose a fuzzy hybrid as a clever third option and answered, "Marse Stickle was fixin' to give me a hint when we was interrupted."

"Man, what the hell gives with this guy?" asked the frustrated disembodied voice of authority.

> *"The celestial ether shall always be blue,*
>
> *And to thee my heart shall ever be true.*
>
> *Moonbeams and lilacs shall brighten thy way,*
>
> *As I guide thee from treetops all of the day."*

Stickle was there, but not there. He was there enough to counsel Eggplant Charlie, but not there enough to have become invisible. By the odor and feeling of breath on his face, Eggplant Charlie could sense Stickle was leaning in to advise him.

"Give it a rest, Mr. Tambo. You're not in the line. Tell the man what he needs to hear," suggested Stickle.

"Give me a hint, sir!" pleaded Eggplant Charlie. "Your music has given me a hint many times before. I need to show these people that I can be in their dimension if I have to. I need to get back to Cauliflower."

Stickle leaned in closer and sang.

> "*Oh I come from Mississippi*
>
> *By way of Tennessee*
>
> *Going back to Tusk- a-loosey,*
>
> *For my gal I need to see.*
>
> *Oh! Alama —bahma*
>
> *Obama —lama Birmingham*
>
> *If you listen to my story,*
>
> *You will know just who I am.*"

"I love that song, Mr. Stickle. Always have."

"Then sing it, son!"

"*Oh! Alama —bahma, Obama —lama Birmingham!*"

"Bingo! He's with us," adjudicated the disembodied voice of authority

Kirk, Scottie, Mr. Bones, Mr. Interlocutor and Stephen Ray Stickle made a conga-line and danced out of Eggplant Charlie's visual field, leaving Eggplant Charlie a problem, one that he couldn't possibly have solved in his current state of mind.

"*If I am dead or dying, what will become of Cauliflower?*"

She was in custody right then, and handcuffed. They tested the blood on her face. It was Eggplant Charlie's, all right. They did to her what those in charge frequently do with people they consider crazy. They gave her drugs.

They injected her with something that they usually give to mass murderers who have been captured alive after a shooting spree. All the cares that she had in the world vanished as if by magic. She wanted to sleep, but they brought her into a special room to answer questions.

"You feeling okay now, hon?" asked the lady in charge.

"Yes, ma'am." She wasn't lying. The drugs were doing their stuff.

"You feel good enough to answer some questions, hon?"

They read Cauliflower her rights, but she was too dopey to understand them.

"Maybe we should let her sleep first," suggested the other cop in the room.

"No, let's find out what the hell happened here," responded boss lady cop. She faced Cauliflower and asked, "Did you stab your old man?"

That question, posed to a person like Cauliflower was simply absurd, and exceedingly humorous. Cauliflower was such a gentle soul that she couldn't set a mousetrap, much less stab a human being. The question would be the equivalent of asking a child if he had eaten his grandmother's shoes.

It provoked the same response, which was unfortunate. Cauliflower laughed hysterically, so she was taken to a mental hospital for observation.

"… **a**s I guide thee from treetops all of the day…." Sam was having disturbing thoughts. Squirrel languages have no future tense, and precious few adverbial phrases, yet this thought occurred to Sam as his little mind engaged in *displacement*, a feature of thought erroneously considered exclusively human by ethologists. He was thinking about another time and place. He was homesick. His trees were not these strange tall pines. He was used to jumping around on swamp maples and sweet gums. His *paisanos* didn't tell him to get lost all the time. He was, after all, *squirrel*, and thereby endowed by nature with certain inalienable rights.

"**M**r. Stickle, where are you?"

"What the hell, man. I ain't Stickle. Are you crazy?" It was Mark Metacomet.

"Mark, where's Cauliflower?"

"You wanna know where's Cauliflower after what she done to you?"

"Where's she at, Mark? I got stuff I need to see her about."

"It was just a joke, you know. I didn't think she'd try to kill you over a stupid song. *Life* and *wife* just rhyme, you know. I thought it was funny 'cause everyone who knows you knows you wouldn't cheat. If I was Miss America, and

I was standing stark-raving bare ass in front of you, you'd still be asking me about Cauliflower. Look man, I'm really, really sorry."

Unfortunately, Mark Metacomet transmogrified into a nude version of Miss America right then, due to power of suggestion, which was greatly amplified in Eggplant Charlie's weakened, trans-dimensional state. This transmogrification was planting thoughts in Eggplant Charlie's mind that were, in their own way, every bit as disturbing as those that forced Sam to grapple with the tense/aspect system of an alien, and oddly internalized, new language.

These disturbing thoughts were, like those of the squirrel, grammatically complex, but that wasn't what bugged Eggplant Charlie about them. The thoughts ran something like this:

"We all know you, Eggplant Charlie, and you are as straight as an arrow, if you are willing to use *straight* as a metaphor for *heterosexual*, and if you can imagine an arrow as the epitome of heterosexuality. However, is this straightness trans-dimensional? Consider the following not-so-hypothetical situation. (… *at this point the voice in Eggplant Charlie's head was a dead ringer for Rod Serling's.)* Your good friend, for whom you are not queer, has just transmogrified himself or has just been transmogrified into a beautiful naked beauty queen. What do you do? How do you feel? Are you a man or a mouse? And, furthermore, what the hell is going on?"

Disturbing thoughts were nothing new to Eggplant Charlie. In fact, he rather enjoyed them. If he had been tying up cucumber vines instead of lying in a hospital room on what was, perhaps, a lesser moon of the planet Saturn, then maybe he would have found the thought amusing. *"Hah, hah, what if Metacomet turned into Miss America and was naked? Would I be queer for him? Ha, hah, hah."*

He wasn't laughing now. You could say, to put it delicately and inaccurately, that he was of two minds right then. What saved him, ironically, was Hollywood. In a Hollywood adaptation of the life of Buddha, there was a scene in which the Buddha was trying to meditate, but these sweet little sexy spirits started dancing naked in front of him. Well, Buddha saw through the crap right quick and told them to get lost, and they revealed their true demonic natures before disappearing. Eggplant Charlie was obviously being put through a test, and he didn't want to fail. Besides, there was what appeared to be some kind of festering pimple on Metacomet/Miss America's… well, let's say upper arm. Focusing on that would make what he had to do next go a lot easier because it was fairly disgusting.

"Mark, it wasn't your fault, and Cauliflower didn't do anything wrong. Could you send Stickle in for me, please? We'll talk more later," said Eggplant Charlie magnanimously.

The pimple burst, spewing pimple pus everywhere. The entire body of whatever/whoever went through the hole opened up by the bursting. What was inside became outside, and it turned out that inside the beauty queen was a fully clothed version of Mark Metacomet.

"All right, I'll go, Eggplant Charlie. But you know hating people for being jerks makes about as much sense as hating trees for losing their leaves," said the demon wearing Mark Metacomet's plaid K-Mart shirt.

"Among the treetops I'll soar and I'll glide, as a cannonball would on a heavenly ride." These, of course, are Stickle's lyrics, but the bard of Orwigsburg's words were appearing, in some strange form, in Sam's brain. There is no squirrel word for *cannonball*, granted, but the rock thrown by Eggplant Charlie gave the concept meaning. *Heavenly*, though, now that was hard to translate into squirrel thought. Squirrels, like humans, can imagine hell much better than they can imagine heaven.

The medieval paintings you see displayed in art museums could have been painted by a squirrel, had the squirrel had opposable thumbs, canvas, pigments… no, that's too much of a stretch. The point is those paintings graphically display all the tortures in store for the damned. But heaven? In the paintings that attempt to portray heaven, paradise looks like the waiting room of a doctor's office, except there are no copies of *Field and Stream*. To the medieval mind, evidently, *heaven* meant the absence of torture.

Of course, that is an inadequate definition. Happiness is more than the lack of unhappiness. Can a person or a squirrel be happy and unhappy at the same time? Are happiness and unhappiness really mutually exclusive? How about heaven and hell? Can they really be defined as opposites in the way that Sam defined *squirrel* and *not-squirrel*?

"In treetops be me squirrel now and near

Now very soon and not soon.

Rolling in special dirt

Beautiful rock

The rock hit me."

Well, that's a relatively poor back translation. It was hard enough for Stickle to do the initial translation into Northeastern Cecil County Squirrel dialect. The reference to "special dirt" was Stickle's attempt to define heaven. Sam once found a large earthenware clay pot into which Cauliflower had put fresh potting soil. Sam rolled in it and was so completely delighted that his inner arbiters elected to move this experience into his long-term memory.

"Beautiful rock," mused Sam. *"Rock of light. Hard not-squirrel. Special not-squirrel. Rolling in special dirt. Rock jumps through light. Light in treetops. Sam is rock."*

All squirrels are, well, squirrely. When they begin thinking the way Sam was thinking, they are prone to running directly under truck tires. Stickle had to monitor the situation. There is a limit to what a squirrel brain can handle all at once.

When he was drawing breath in the realm of squirrels and human beings, Stickle was a pathetic drunk. His lot was an odd combination of fame and poverty. Everyone knew who he was because his songs were sung everywhere.

However, back then, the only time the songwriter would earn money would be when he sold his song to a publisher. The sheet music would get printed, but there were no royalties. What's more, there was plenty of blatant piracy, so even when Stickle sold his song to an honest publisher, it would be plagiarized and resold in short order.

Virtually every hotel and public house in America had sheet music of Stickle's songs. The songs were, and still are, magical, but few people understood what went into them. Stickle was a white guy from a free state, but a free state with a southern exposure. The most popular kinds of entertainment back then were minstrel shows. By today's standards, they were crude and racist, but they appealed to the northern white public's curiosity about an exotic population of which they knew very little-- African-Americans.

Stickle was a rare bird in that he was a musical and lyrical genius who also had a great deal of compassion for his fellow human beings. Not all of his songs were written in Northern boarding houses. He traveled the South to get a true feeling for what he was writing. Being a compassionate soul, he soon realized something. The people on whom the minstrel characters were based were, in fact, real people, and they were every bit as human as Stickle and the members of the audience at the minstrel shows.

He met them. They included enslaved longshoremen, carpenters, and coopers as well as the unskilled farm workers usually called to mind when one ponders American slavery. He wasn't an abolitionist *per se*; he just saw suffering people—people with backs scarred from whippings, people in fear and sorrow at slave auctions as their families were being torn apart before their eyes. He would talk to these people and listen to their stories of family members whom they would never see again.

He hated all that, but he also sought it out. He wrote about it and set it to music, and this element of compassion made his minstrel songs different from the others of his time. They were really about being human, so his white audience could relate to his black characters. They were about the grief and homesickness caused by the forced relocations after slave sales. However, these songs resonated in the hearts of those whites who left their homes and moved west, more often out of desperation than a sense of adventure. Both whites and blacks knew death and grief. Parents lost children to childhood diseases, husbands and children lost wives and mothers to childbirth, and widows and orphans lost husbands and fathers to industrial and agricultural accidents. The songs were also about the joys and disappointments of winning at the racetrack and losing at the cockpit. Everyone could relate. Times were hard. As white folks suffered more as times got harder, they began to suspect that their whiteness was relative, rather than absolute, and that it could conceivably be revoked someday.

Before Harriet Beecher Stowe wrote *Uncle Tom's Cabin*, Stickle had already poisoned the Northern white mind with humanity, and had managed to play a part in the moral salvation of the whole country.

While he was doing this, however, he was still a pathetic drunk. He never had much cash, but when people learned who he was, they were eager to buy him drinks. His attempts at abstinence were all miserable failures. The alcohol helped blunt the pain of the empathy he felt and ease the reality of a life spent on the road at a time when the road was a truly miserable place.

One day, as the War Between the States was in full swing, Stickle stepped out onto the balcony of his third floor boarding house room in western Pennsylvania. He was already plenty pickled, and he didn't really need the drink that he was preparing to nip from his flask. He never took it, either. The wooden railing on the balcony was rotten. He stumbled and fell through it and ended up impaled on the wrought iron fence below. He died instantly.

Stickle had recognized his demons just as Eggplant Charlie recognized the transmogrified image of Mark Metacomet as a demon, but he was not as successful in dismissing them. His tunes charmed heaven itself, and since he had somehow managed to change the world for the better, he was released from the cycle of rebirth. He wasn't off the hook entirely, though. Like a Buddha, he could travel through, and transcend, dimensions. Unlike a Buddha, he carried a lot of baggage as he traveled.

"It's hard for an old drunk like me to enlighten a squirrel," he mused out loud. He thought of himself as old even though he had died before the age of forty. He actually had had a relatively long life for a chemically dependent proto-rock star.

In heaven, it is said that there are beings who volunteer to return to Earth. Can you imagine that? Why would they? The answer is that they are so full of compassion and that they are so distressed by the evil in the world that they want to help. They forgo an eternity of rolling in special dirt for an opportunity to help out. This is very risky business. They are born with no memory, and all the pitfalls that can bring an enlightened being down to a cretinous level await them, perhaps to re-trap them in an endless cycle of death and rebirth. They cannot choose their skin color, nationality, gender, social status or level of intelligence. These things are chosen for them, often with the aim of sending the right person to the right place at the right time.

Cauliflower sure seemed to have been in the wrong place at the wrong time. Now she was shackled to a bed and "high" if you can call being in a drug-induced stupor "high", all for the crime of laughing at the absurdity of the suggestion that she had stabbed her favorite human being.

"She exhibits the classic symptoms," said the doctor leading a group of interns. The doctor spoke as if Cauliflower were not really there, but for all their attempts to shackle her with chemicals and straps, Cauliflower was, in fact, just about all there.

"Inappropriateness of affect, for example," continued the doctor. "When confronted with the fact that she had stabbed her husband, she broke out laughing."

Cauliflower became angry, which was rare for her. It was also unusual for "patients" who had been administered the cocktail of medications she had received to be angry, sad, or happy, or much of anything in the emotional realm.

"*I didn't stab Eggplant Charlie! I don't know how he cut himself!*" is what she wanted to say.

"Mynwabyegplancharl. Nynyooweecultemsef," is what she uttered.

The interns were glad she was chained to the bed because, despite their advanced educations, the majority of them suspected that they were witnessing a genuine case of demonic possession.

Eggplant Charlie wasn't chained to his bed. He didn't have to be. In his current state, he didn't have the strength to swat a fly. Mr. Bones entered the room.

"Mr. Bones, are we in the line? Where's Mr. Interlocutor?"

Mr. Bones didn't smile. He was wearing his Starfleet uniform and carrying a medical tricorder.

"It's just Bones, not Mr. Bones. I'm a doctor, damn it. And I'm only "Bones" to my friends. You can call me Dr. McCoy."

"And I is Dr. Tambo. Might I inquires where am Dr. Interlocutor?"

Bones was not amused. Kirk was not around, and neither was Scottie; just Bones, and Bones was grouchier than Eggplant Charlie on a bad day. Eggplant Charlie had never noticed it before, but Bones was jet black. He had never remembered the grouchy, virulently anti-Vulcan country doctor from Mississippi as being black before.

"How am I, doctor?"

"Yeah, that's better. Well, you've lost a lot of that red stuff you call blood, and your heart is where your liver should be, but aside from that, at least as far as I can tell, you're fine."

"Can I have visitors?"

"Sure, I don't see why not. Who do you want to see? The woman who bit you half to death?"

The last comment just kind of went by Eggplant Charlie. The doctor obviously hated him. For some reason, he seemed to think that Eggplant Charlie was a Vulcan. No matter.

"I really want to see Stephen Ray Stickle," said Eggplant Charlie.

"Well, I really want to see Scott Joplin, but your people locked him up in a nuthouse. I really want to see Bessie Smith, but she was denied treatment at one of your hospitals. You wanna see Stephen Ray Stickle. Well that's just fine. No problem, except he's as dead as dead can be. What's wrong with you? Has your `superior' logic suddenly gone haywire?" He shook his head as he left the room.

Eggplant Charlie felt his face with his hands. There were stitches everywhere. What a strange texture.

"*A strange and delightful texture,*" thought Sam, more or less and in a process involving some burdensome circumlocution, as he rolled in a pile of pine needles. "*Heavenly!*"

Mark Metacomet was into the third of four forty five minute sets. The house was packed with co-op people eager to hear the songs Mark made up about them. Last Saturday night, the subject was Bertha the Lesbian Roofer.

Notice that the *L* in lesbian and the *R* in roofer are both capitalized. This was the handle by which she introduced herself. This was also what she painted on the side of her trucks, all ten of them. She had a reputation for being the best roofer in the tri-state area, and business was thriving. Now, you might wonder how such a person would not only survive but prevail in the roughest of the building trades, and that story would take quite some time to relate, but, in a nutshell, Bertha the Lesbian Roofer was as tough as nails, took no crap from anyone, and had zero tolerance for phoniness of any sort. No one knew exactly where she lived, maybe somewhere between Rising Sun and Havre De Grace, and no one had ever met her significant other, to whom she referred as her "husband." Well, everybody talks about everybody behind their backs, and people used to speculate about her mysterious husband. The mystery was that Bertha was about as macho as any human could possibly be, so how could she be the more feminine half of a couple? Mark Metacomet, to his dubious credit, was the first person to speculate on this, right in front of her and the rest of the co-op crowd, in a song he wrote to the tune of *Buffalo Gals*. The members of the audience would glance at Bertha to see if it was okay for them to laugh and enjoy the song. Bertha didn't crack a smile. They waited to see if Bertha would kill Mark at the end of the song. She was, after all, an ex-con, as were many of the members of her roofing crews. Finally, when the song was over, Bertha shouted, "Haw, haw! That was great. You got some stones, there, Mark Metacomet!" The audience went wild. It was quite a performance as all the tension in the room was released at once. What the audience didn't know was that Mark Metacomet and Bertha had arranged it all in advance. Bertha really enjoyed scaring people in general, and earth hippies in particular, so she was more than willing to play along and be a good sport. Anyway, that was last week.

Lilith Borden sat at a table, nursing her vodka and tonic. Lilith was one of the very few people who really didn't like Cauliflower. She actually *hated* Cauliflower. She worked with Cauliflower at the co-op and was disgusted with how ditzy and useless she seemed to be and disgusted with how tolerant everyone else seemed to be of her incompetence. Lilith didn't hate Eggplant Charlie, but she was, like a lot of his acquaintances, afraid of him. She detested what she saw as Cauliflower's dependence on Eggplant Charlie, but she was blind to the fact, as were most folks who knew them, that Eggplant Charlie was equally dependent on Cauliflower.

Lilith loved ratting out Cauliflower to anyone who would listen. "It took her five minutes to make change for a dollar!" or "She stacked the honey jars in a pyramid! What a stupid waste of space!" That last comment was a bit ambiguous, and that ambiguity was, unbeknownst to Lilith, a bit of demonic word play. Demons, in addition to being miserable bastards, are all natural poets.

Lilith was oblivious to the fact that complaining about a person as popular as Cauliflower was not making her many friends. She was only vaguely aware that her character assassination attempts would be futile as long as Eggplant Charlie was a local celebrity.

Lilith was delighted when the video went viral. Now everyone could see what a whacko Cauliflower was, and maybe Eggplant Charlie wouldn't survive the attack. A girl can dream, can't she? She could assume her rightful position as queen of the co-op, and, under her direction, it would run like clockwork. She would be the Mussolini of organic produce.

Redneck Davey was sipping his beer nervously. He was really hoping Mark Metacomet wouldn't target him tonight. He was low man on the totem pole in Bertha the Lesbian Roofer's business, and most of his many bosses were women who were manlier than he was. Redneck Davey didn't like his new handle when he first got it at the co-op. He was a transplant to Cecil County from East Tennessee, so he had actually only moved from the heart of the South to its northeastern fringe, but his *patois* was so colloquial that it made Minnie Pearl seem cosmopolitan by comparison. People teased him at the co-op, where he worked on weekends, about his accent, and his reaction to this was to avoid speaking entirely unless it was absolutely necessary.

When he first got hired by Bertha, this tendency to be taciturn earned him points. In the building trades, keeping one's mouth shut is seen as a very positive thing. The women on the crew called him "baby" or "honey child" at first, which he didn't like much. Then, one day Eggplant Charlie was working alongside him as a favor to Bertha-- tradespeople are a little like doctors in that they often swap services with no exchange of cash—and he needed some more nails. "Yo, Redneck Davey!" He called. "Get me some one-and-a-quarter-inch roofers!" The gals on the job thought the new handle was cute and catchy, so they started calling the new laborer 'Redneck Davey', too. This came as relief to Redneck Davey, who was sick and tired of being called 'baby'.

Redneck Davey was actually very sensitive about a lot of things, including being very sensitive. Mark Metacomet could crush his soul with one unkind lyric. The shy Tennessean was bracing himself, trying to find strength through a combination of prayer and Pabst Blue Ribbon. "Lord, if it must come," he prayed, "thy will be done, but let it be tonight, for I am ready."

Lilith had had a victorious week. The people she perceived as her enemies were either in the I.C.U. or the nuthouse, and she was feeling fine. "Play a song about Cauliflower!" Lilith hollered at Mark Metacomet.

"Woah, ho, well, let's see what we got here."

Then, to the tune of "John Hardy", Mark Metacomet sang:

> *"Cauliflower, she was a sweet lady so fine,*
>
> *But she sharpened her teeth every day,*
>
> *She bit Eggplant Charlie on the Delaware state line,*
>
> *And I seen Cauliflower gettin' away,*
>
> *'Where's my squirrel?'*
>
> *I seen Cauliflower gettin' away."*

Lilith laughed raucously, and her laughter made Mark Metacomet feel a bit ashamed. Eggplant Charlie had been good to him, and he actually liked Cauliflower a lot. Furthermore, he had been shocked, rather than amused, at what Cauliflower had supposedly done, yet here he was, singing a rather mean little song for no apparent reason. But there *was* a reason. Lilith knew what it was, and so did Mark Metacomet. Mark wanted Lilith, and this little ditty might have just closed the deal. That would have been okay with Lilith.

Lilith had decided a long time ago that she hated men, mostly for political reasons. She wanted to be a radical feminist lesbian separatist and live completely independently of males. The problem was that she really wasn't a lesbian, and her lesbian friends and acquaintances knew it. After Lilith had foolishly tried to flirt with Bertha the Lesbian Roofer, the czarina of thirty-year shingles called her a "phony-ass bitch", and threatened to sic her "husband" on her, but, of course, Bertha had an appetite for scaring folks.

Her more compassionate lesbian friends simply lost patience with her insincere and rather pathetic come-ons, and held what today would be called an intervention, but what at the time just seemed to be an ambush.

"You know, pretending to be a lesbian is just like pretending to be an Indian or Black or disabled, Lilith. It really isn't cool at all." And so on. It was a rough evening, but it took the phony wind out of Lilith's sails.

Of course, she had mainly been lying to herself, so now she had to come clean. Okay. She needed these jerks, but for one thing, and one thing only.

Mark Metacomet looked like he could fulfill that particular need, at least for this week, so she let him know that she was delighted with his trashing of Cauliflower, even as other co-op people were walking out in disgust.

Lilith had a name which was similar to Eggplant Charlie's in that she wasn't born with it. Her first name was taken from the legend of Adam's first wife, who, unlike Eve, was not submissive, and who, unlike Eve, was made from earth rather than from a hunk of Adam's bone tissue. Her adopted surname was borrowed from Lizzie Borden, who had earned Lilith's admiration by bludgeoning her father with an axe.

Mark Metacomet, by the way, was really named Mark Metacomet at birth, and he really was descended from King Phillip, though few people believed it.

Mark Metacomet wanted to live up to his name and go beyond being a mere shooting star. Ah, How wondrous to be *Metacomet* streaking across the August sky, putting the Northern Lights to shame. Well, here he was in a little bar in a small city in the Mid-Atlantic, singing for audiences that numbered from two or three to thirty or forty. It looked as though he had finally found a groupie, though, so, at the end of the set, he politely asked Lilith if he could sit down. Lilith replied with a dazzling smile and a laugh. "I think you're wonderful," she said.

"**T**his is a real dog," said the D.A. "You shoulda read her her rights before they gave her the dope."

"We did what we thought we had to do. I'm sorry," said the lady cop. "But she's as crazy as can be and I don't think the jury'll let 'er walk."

"I sure as hell hope not. We coulda gotten guilty but mentally ill. Now, we're stuck with not guilty by reason of insanity and we're at the mercy of the damn head docs."

"I'm sure they'll keep her there, ma'am. She's under observation right now. I heard that she scared a whole bunch of interns just by growling at 'em. They was pretty glad she was cuffed to the bed."

Rolling in pine needles after falling from the tree tops gave Sam a taste of heaven. However, he was awakened from this bliss by the stares of a number of strange squirrels from this neck of the woods.

"What? What? What?" asked one squirrel. Sam found this lingo was close enough to his dialect for him to understand.

Sam answered physically, rather than verbally, by rolling in the pine needles.

"Why? Why?" These clicked words were also comprehensible to Sam. They were usually used by females to reject suitors.

"Why not? Why not?" clicked Sam. These words were usually used in response to rejections from females.

"Rolling in special dirt" clicked Sam, but they couldn't understand his clicks. They could understand his *meaning,* however, and thirteen clicks followed by five quick clicks quickly became the word for *heavenly* in the dialect of Cecil County Squirrel spoken in the woods behind the vet's office.

> "*Rolling in special dirt*
>
> *Rock hit me Sam squirrel*
>
> *Hard not-squirrel hit*
>
> *Sam Squirrel.*
>
> *Not —squirrel squirrel is now*
>
> *Squirrel is squirrels*
>
> *Rolling in special dirt.*"

Damn! Stickle's head hurt. *Enough squirrel talk.* Maybe he had finally gone crazy. Why mess with a bunch of silly rodents? He needed a break from the goofy little bushy-tailed rats. No, that's unkind. It's no more accurate to call a squirrel a rat than it is to call a human a baboon. *Well,* Stickle thought. *I might as well get back to the baboons. There's work to be done there, too.*

There was no A.A. when Stickle was alive, and every hotel was also a bar. Furthermore, he was literally the toast of the town in every town he visited. Attempts at abstinence were always very short lived. Even if he could swear off for an hour or two, they always got him in the end, and every night that he spent on the road, he went to bed drunk. The only hangover cure for him was a nip on the old flask, so Stickle was a dill pickle when he inhabited the realm of mortals and immortals.

"The Immortal Stephen Ray Stickle," he read aloud as he walked past a record store on Main Street and observed a prominently displayed c.d. collection. "Performed by today's artists," he continued.

Well, the town had certainly changed, but The Old Post Road Tavern was still here. There was a sign on the door advertising *Mark Metacomet and King Phillip's Revenge.* Stickle put two and two together and realized that this would be the entertainment for tonight.

He used to stop here overnight while traveling from Baltimore to Philadelphia. It looked vaguely familiar. The customers were dressed differently, of course. The clothes looked more comfortable. In addition, unlike the situation in the old days, there were as many, if not more, women in the place as men, and since he had always enjoyed the company of women, Stickle approved of the changes.

Stickle thought hard about what he had to do. Thank heaven he could still nip a gin while he pondered his next move. This dimension wasn't heaven, and it wasn't hell, but liquor seemed endlessly available, just as it was in his traveling days.

The problem with communicating with squirrels was that their language was so stilted and bizarre. It reflected their culture, which was quite different from Stickle's. After his demise, he had kept his culture along with his gin, and, like the gin, it was both heavenly and hellish.

Stickle could appear to the humans in this dimension rather easily, but doing so would be very wrong. "Ghosts", as they are sometimes called, break the laws of the universe when they decide to appear like holograms to ordinary people. This causes a lot of confusion, and more importantly, it's a major distraction. Shakespeare's play *Hamlet* has been analyzed to death, but one element of the play that the living have all missed, but to which the dead are all painfully hip, is the unintended damage that Hamlet's father did to his son by simply appearing to him.

"This world is for the living," Stickle reminded himself aloud.

"You say something?" asked one bar patron to another.

"No, man. You're hearing things," responded another.

Stickle caught himself. It was just an absent-minded mishap, and he was a drunk, after all. "*Keep your thoughts to yourself, you old drunk,*" he thought silently.

Stickle could appear to people who were considered delusional by the authorities, or people who were not expected to think clearly. Thus, he could be himself around Eggplant Charlie, which was delightful because he liked Eggplant Charlie. However, when you are on a mission, or on several missions as Stickle was, you need to watch your delights. They can be distracting. It would be pleasant to spend more time with Eggplant Charlie, and Eggplant Charlie would surely appreciate the company, but his mission involved enlightening squirrels and jerks like Mark Metacomet.

Stickle couldn't just walk up to a walking, talking turkey like Mark Metacomet in his stinky suit with the grimy, over-sized bow-tie and announce that he was a long-dead composer with an important message to relate.

Transmogrification was a very unattractive option, although it was not technically a violation of the rules. Demons transmogrified all the time, and Stickle detested demons. He was aware that there was a demon who lived in his flask, and that he could not or would not expel that particular one, but he really detested that demon, too, perhaps because that was the demon to which he was most attached.

It is both extremely easy and extremely foolhardy to attach oneself to a demon, but people do it all the time. Eggplant Charlie was able to see through the transmogrification and send the Metacomet/Miss America demon packing, but there were others around him that he couldn't get rid of so easily.

Cauliflower had no problems with demons. They couldn't even look at her. In their dimension, looking at directly at Cauliflower would be like trying to observe solar flares with the naked eye in ours.

Demons didn't care about Sam. By their lights, he was just a stupid squirrel. Demons rarely possessed animals or attached themselves to them, as they were stymied by the same kinds of things that stymied Stickle as he sought to telepathically influence Sam. Demons are not immune to headaches and they are real crybabies when it comes to any form of pain.

Lilith wasn't a demon, but she had foolishly attached herself to a number of them. She took her first name from one, and she took her surname from a tormented individual, which attracted the demons that had caused the torment. Lilith sat at her table at The Old Post Road Tavern, waiting for Mark Metacomet to finish his set. The demons of spite, hate, envy lust and anger were palpable to most of the tavern-goers as bad vibes. Customers moved away from her, and many of them walked out on Mark Metacomet's set as he was trashing Cauliflower.

From Stickle's multi-dimensional perspective, the bad vibes were actually repulsive demons sitting at Lilith's table. He looked at the mess at her table the same way that an exterminator looks at a kitchen crawling with cockroaches.

"I've got my work cut out for me," he said. People heard him, but they weren't listening. Stickle looked at Lilith with pity. She wasn't the trap; she was only the bait. He needed to distract Mark Metacomet before he sat next to Lilith Borden Cheese Food Product.

He needed to talk to Metacomet alone, away from Lilith, whom he could try to fix later. He decided that the only place he could talk to him alone would be the men's room. He sent a telepathic signal to Mark Metacomet.

"You need to go to the bathroom."

That one was easy. Almost any "ghost" can send that signal successfully to almost any man, woman, child or beast. Anything more complicated than that requires a lot more effort, and the signal is likely to be garbled.

Mark Metacomet leaned into the microphone and said, "I'll be right back." He winked at Lilith, an action which he instantly regretted as it was a cheesy gesture, but, to his delight, she smiled and winked back. He was going to get some Lilith tonight, or so he thought, and the endorphins started buzzing around his brain like fireflies.

Transmogrification, Yuck! It was a tall order for a dead old drunk. He could only say a few words to Mark

Metacomet, and then he'd have to run. For a poor old dead drunk like Stickle, holding a shape together for one minute would be the equivalent of an emphysema patient holding his breath for three minutes.

Stickle walked into the bathroom and went into an empty stall to transmogrify. He could have made himself appear as a college student, an earth hippie from the co-op, a faculty member or a construction worker. To whom would Mark Metacomet be most inclined to listen? The mousetrap, baited with Lilith, would still be there after Mark Metacomet finished his bodily business. How to persuade the mouse not to linger by Lilith the limburger? The mousetrap metaphor was a little overwhelming, so Stickle couldn't think straight in the short time that he had.

Mark Metacomet entered the rest room, unzipped his fly, and approached the urinal. He heard the stall door open behind him, and he heard a voice.

"Mark Metacomet?"

"Huh?" he turned around quickly despite himself, and he peed a little on his shoes.

"Are you a man or a mouse?"

Stickle had transmogrified himself into a giant mouse— not like Mickey Mouse, not like Mighty Mouse. Stickle looked exactly like a mouse that one might see on a kitchen counter, sniffling, whiskers shaking a bit, but this mouse was six feet tall and could talk.

Mark Metacomet screamed and ran out of the rest room without tucking his business back in his pants. He didn't stop to pick up his guitar or talk to Lilith. He ran as if he had been fifteen years younger, all the way down Main Street, until he caught the attention of some cops and two amateur cellphone cinematographers.

It worked. The mouse disappeared. It was all Stickle could do to hold it together for fifteen seconds. Stickle, once again invisible to the dwellers of Mark Metacomet's dimension, staggered into the tavern area –it wasn't the first time—and collapsed into the seat next to Lilith and her demons.

Lilith was looking around, but she didn't rise from her seat. She could have sworn that she had just seen Mark Metacomet run through the bar with his business out and flapping about. She had definitely heard a scream.

"Everything's okay, folks," said the bartender after looking in the bathroom. "Guy musta had too many shots."

It couldn't have been Mark Metacomet after all. There he was, sitting next to her! The expression on his face was one of complete calm. Lilith had never noticed this before, but Mark Metacomet smelled like body odor and gin.

"Lilith, can I ask you a question?"

"What just happened?"

"Gee, I don't know, but can I ask you a question?"

"Sure. Go ahead."

"Would you still come home with me if I were a naked beauty pageant winner?"

Lilith threw the remains of her drink in what she thought was Mark Metacomet's face and walked out. Stickle relaxed and disappeared. A ghost's disappearing is remarkably unnoticeable unless you are looking for it. A ghost's appearing is quite unsettling, however. Anyway, no one noticed when Stickle let Mark Metacomet's form disintegrate. He sat back, completely invisible once again, relaxed, took a nip and chuckled at his own jokes.

"All squirrels are squirrel. No squirrels are not squirrel. Sam squirrel is squirrel. Sam squirrel is all squirrel. All squirrels are Sam squirrel. Rolling in special dirt!"

Sam was chattering away at his new pals, but they didn't care much. They had already learned what they thought he had to teach. They were rolling in pine needles, and as their little bodies snapped the more brittle needles, a sweet aroma was released. They were all rolling away, mostly silently, but there was some chattering.

Squirrels aren't much like people in that they don't glorify the teacher, the master, the guru, the rabbi or whatever you want to call the sentient being that plays that role. The teacher is just squirrel; the important thing is the lesson. Sam was just a squirrel among squirrels, slightly handicapped by the language barrier and the loss of equilibrium caused by his head trauma. Nevertheless, this was a change for the better, for now he was *squirrel*, rather than *not-squirrel*, in the eyes of his new *companeros*.

"How are we doing today? Can you say anything? We thought we had lost you yesterday. You were losing a lot of blood."

Eggplant Charlie couldn't remember the name of the actress in the white lab coat. She was mighty pretty, though. Mighty like a rose. Long jet black hair and glasses. Straight out of central casting.

"Come off it Mark," said Eggplant Charlie. "Send Stickle back in."

"You keep asking for Stickle. Who or what is Stickle?"

"The only one I'm pretty sure is real," replied Eggplant Charlie. "Not Mr. Bones, not Mr. Interlocutor, not Captain Kirk, not Miss America and not you."

"You don't think I'm real?"

"You're a figment of my loss of blood."

"How do you know?"

"Look at you! The perfect nerd-princess ultra feminine doctor. Straight out of Hollywood!"

"Gee, thanks, I guess, but I assure you that I'm real."

The doctor smiled at Eggplant Charlie's slightly snide comment, which to Eggplant Charlie seemed to say, "*Go ahead and call me Barbie. I'm a figment. It doesn't hurt.*" This didn't mean that Eggplant Charlie was in any way inclined to experiment with more snide remarks; it simply meant *no harm, no foul.* If he was really talking to a figment of his imagination, then he was really talking to a part of himself, and there was no point in being nasty to himself.

Eggplant Charlie was kind of pleased that one part of himself looked like this. The fact that this part was a beautiful woman didn't bother him at all. Eggplant Charlie may have been "straight as an arrow", if you pardon that bizarre metaphor, but he had always enjoyed certain androgynous pursuits such as sewing, and even knitting. He was aware of having a feminine side, and if his feminine side looked like this, so much the better.

"You know, I like you a lot better than Doctor McCoy. I don't like the part of me that hates Vulcans, but I'm tickled pink that you're in me, and I'm in you."

The doctor's brow furrowed. Where was the dazzling smile now? If she were part of Eggplant Charlie, he ought to be able to control her facial expression.

"Come on, pretty me-doctor Barbie-Eggplant Charlie. Smile again! I want to see it! I'm not asking you/me to do anything weird, though it has crossed my mind," he said out loud. Why not? Talking to oneself out loud is fine. Contrary to a lot of goofy conventional wisdom, it is not a sign of insanity or feeble-mindedness.

The doctor looked even more concerned now. *Inappropriate behavior. Head trauma again. Where was it coming from? The x-rays showed no sign…*

"Sir, don't feel bad about saying these things to me. I know you don't mean them. I know you're not yourself right now. We'll talk later."

Eggplant Charlie realized that he had done something seriously wrong, and he felt the heaviness of guilt, but he had no idea why.

"I'm sorry!" He blurted. Here he was apologizing to his feminine side! He needed to say something or this wonderful part of himself would get offended and leave the room, and he wanted the company, real or unreal.

"Who's the president of the United States?" He called out to the doctor.

"Are you asking me?" she said.

"Why not. That's what everyone was asking me. I couldn't remember. Stickle gave me the answer."

"Umhmm. Interesting. Stickle again."

She was so cute, it made Eggplant Charlie queasy.

"So Ms. Figment….."

"That's Doctor Figment," she said, correcting Eggplant Charlie and giggling a bit.

"Whatever. You gonna answer?"

"Why don't you tell me. I'm trying to see how you are doing, and answering that question would be a good start."

> *"Oh I come from Mississippi*
>
> *By way of Tennessee*
>
> *Going back to Tusk-a-loosey*
>
> *My ebon lover for to see.*
>
> *O ! Alama- bama*
>
> *O-bama-lama Birmingham*
>
> *Listen closely to my story*
>
> *And you'll know just who I am."*

"Very nice!" She giggled again. Sweet as pie. Who was worse, angels or demons? He had important business to take care of, and this bespectacled beauty was an annoying, yet attractive, distraction.

"Ooh, and you're very nice, too," countered grumpy-ass Eggplant Charlie. The smile left her face as his new tone registered with her.

"You're showing symptoms of head trauma, but there is no sign of concussion. Did your wife hit you over the head with something before she....?"

"Huh? Who? Cauliflower? Are you talking about Cauliflower beating me over the head?"

Doctor Cutie Pie's expression changed to one of serious concern. *The patient is delusional, but there is no real explanation for it. His utterance, which evokes the image of the vegetable cauliflower bludgeoning him, was probably indicative of aphasia. Is the patient worried about his own deteriorating condition? Is he worried about becoming a "vegetable"? In addition to biting and perhaps stabbing him, what else has that deranged woman done to this man? How long has this abuse been going on?*

"Mister…what can I call you?"

"Mr. Tambo, if I am to be in the line."

"Mr. Tambeaux, how long have you been the victim of spousal abuse?"

"Cauliflower is the purest soul on the face of the Earth, Doctor Barbie. Where is Kirk?"

The doctor's face changed again. It didn't transmogrify. She didn't turn into a giant mouse. She just winced. Being called "Doctor Barbie" had somehow offended her, and it registered on her face. Eggplant Charlie felt the way he had after he thought he had put that squirrel's lights out.

"I'm sorry. My face hurts," he said.

"That's okay." The doctor thought that Eggplant Charlie might be making progress, and if that were the case, and if these delusions were just a temporary, albeit unusual, symptom of blood loss rather than a sign of mysterious head trauma, then the prognosis would be much better. She smiled at Eggplant Charlie to reassure him that she took no offense. Unfortunately, Eggplant Charlie took that as a signal that she really was a figment, and, therefore, had no real feelings to hurt.

Eggplant Charlie's occasional meanness was usually followed up by remorse. It was usually the result of letting his grouchiness get the best of him and allowing it to morph into something uglier. '*Damn Squirrel!*' morphed into a perfectly pointed projectile, and ' *Friggin' figment!*' turned into a barb which suggested that his feminine side was nothing more than a plastic toy.

What was wrong with a human being being beautiful or handsome, anyway? Eggplant Charlie didn't think of himself as being particularly hung up on looks either way. Men who preened and wore expensive duds didn't bother him as long as they bought his produce or left him alone. When he was younger, he had had trouble looking drop-dead-gorgeous women, like the doctor, in the eye. They had been, to Eggplant Charlie, what Cauliflower was to demons—bright suns, impossible to look at directly for any period of time. He got over this bashfulness later in life by focusing on their personality flaws. This brought home the fact that they were human, after all, and simply potential purchasers of produce, sellers of software, and the like. They belched and farted and shat and had their odiferous moments like everybody else. He had also noticed, back when he was single, that many of these beautiful women were profoundly lonely. To his amazement, when he worked up the nerve to ask some out, he had about a fifty percent success rate.

Cauliflower had been different, though. One morning at the farmer's market, she approached his stand, smiled, and asked him to go with her to the Old Post Road Inn for open mic night. From that moment on, his space would be permanently invaded and occupied by a life-giving sun. Eggplant Charlie became a true eggplant, getting all his energy and *raison d'etre* by way of photosynthesis.

Cauliflower, the sun which nourished the eggplant, lay shackled to a bed, drowsy and nauseous from the psycho-active substances the medical professionals had injected into her system. Those who confused sweetness with weakness or confused purity with stupidity always underestimated Cauliflower. Like the sun, she radiated energy…well, we all do, but less cynical sentient beings, even squirrels like Sam, could feel their own power being fueled by her very presence.

Shackled and doped as she was, she was also accumulating a stockpile of righteous anger, because even though the dope they had given her could pacify a raging bull, it ultimately did not have the power to contain the fury of a good woman who had been falsely accused of a horrible crime. Her muscles were lax now, not tense. Her thoughts were relatively clear, although they would not necessarily be decipherable to most people, and her soul was oddly at peace, for she knew that *now was not the time*. She was recharging, and the light had not turned green yet --recharging so that she could get back to the business of *being*. This was clearly no place to *be*. She also was aware of the fact that Eggplant Charlie needed her. He was evidently pretty uncomfortable somewhere now, and she really was concerned.

Stickle was disgusted. In the woods behind the vet's office, he was observing a spectacle that would have won a wildlife photographer a prize, but Stickle was no photographer, and what he saw just reinforced his pessimistic feeling that enlightening squirrels was a fool's errand.

They were rolling in pine needles, chattering away, clicking "special dirt" in Sam's language, a phrase which had come to mean "pine needles on the forest floor" in the dialect that could be called Woods Behind State Line Veterinarians' Squirrel. Stickle, in his current condition, was blessed, or cursed, with the telepathic ability to understand all squirrel dialects, but it wasn't as much fun, as it would have been for, say, Doctor Doolittle, because in reality, squirrel thoughts are--sorry--squirrelly.

The squirrels had confused pine needles with heaven. They had taken the metaphor literally and were now trying to reach heaven by rolling in pine needles. The mission seemed hopeless. It was true that Sam, with whom Stickle had tried to communicate one-on-one through telepathic means, was a little more enlightened than the others, but there was no way that Stickle could bring the concept of heaven to each and every squirrel. Unfortunately, one squirrel would have to enlighten the other, and it seemed as though this process would be like a game of "whisper down the line", with the message becoming increasingly muddled, garbled and dumbed down as it passed from rodent to rodent.

The problem, as Stickle understood it, was, in part, a language problem. Sam had been able to teach this nation of squirrels to roll in pine needles, and this much they had learned. Since they had no "word" for this activity in their language, they borrowed a "phrase" from Sam's, which had originally meant "rolling in special dirt." Now, however, they were just rolling, and Sam was chattering away as they rolled, oblivious to the fact that none of these foreign squirrels really understood him, and foolishly elated at the fact that the squirrels behind the vet's office had taken to rolling, which he took as confirmation that they had really understood him.

There he was, chattering away about his concept of heaven! What a guru! Sam had only caught a nanosecond long glimpse of a dimension from a thought telepathically communicated to him metaphorically by a long-dead drunken songwriter who had been excluded from entering the kingdom himself due to his drunkenness. Now, this audacious squirrel felt qualified to preach!

Actually, Sam's qualifications were about as solid as those of most humans in the preaching business, but Stickle was not irked at them. He was pissed off at the little squirrel because he had attached himself to Sam, so Sam now had the ability to disappoint him. Stickle had also attached himself to the ultimate failure or success of the mission instead of focusing on the mission itself, so he was failing.

"Rolling in special dirt!

Copulation!

Acorns, acorns and acorns!

You are squirrel and me/Sam is squirrel

No squirrel is not squirrel!

All squirrel is me/Sam!

Sam is all squirrel.

You are all Sam squirrel.

Roll, squirrel, Roll!"

Sam's chattering almost made ghostly Stickle pick up a ghostly rock and peg it, as Eggplant Charlie had done so disastrously with a three dimensional rock, at Sam's little head. That would have been within Stickle's range of powers, but Stickle had been walking a thin line lately.

Stickle was no Buddha, nor was he any kind of messiah. He was not among the class of beings who had decided to return to earth to help humanity. He was a "ghost", one who was on probation but who had earned temporary dispensation from the cycle of rebirth, a kind of dispensation granted to certain humans, who, although flawed, had somehow been able to make the realm of mortals and immortals, commonly known as Planet Earth, a better place. There were many of his kind. They all provided guidance to all who drew breath, human and animal, but since they were not perfect beings because they hadn't released all their attachments, their guidance could, at times, mislead rather than enlighten.

These righteous ghosts are not as prone to succumbing to the weaknesses of the flesh as are those who draw breath because they have no real flesh, at least not in the three-dimensional realm. They can still succumb to other weaknesses, though, and often the so-called weaknesses of the flesh are really symptomatic of flaws that are more than skin deep.

A "Ghost" like Stickle was always at risk of becoming a demon. Using one's ghostly power to transmogrify oneself was a stupid demonic trick, but in the case of Stickle's transmogrification into a mouse at the Old Post Road Inn, it could be forgiven as a temporary lapse in taste or as a desperate move. However, doing it again just to clean up the atmosphere around Lilith's table and perhaps just to amuse himself might well have sent Stickle tumbling into the spiritual abyss of demonhood, a descent which would have made his fatal fall from the boarding house balcony seem like a dive into a cool refreshing lake if his celestial parole officers had been paying closer attention.

Stickle felt a great deal of guilt and self-loathing as he heard Sam chatter. The self-loathing, which had been displaced so that it turned into an aggressive impulse directed at Sam, was adding to his guilt because he had really been thinking of throwing a trans-dimensional stone at Sam's already traumatized head.

"What a foul spirit I am! I need a drink!" Stickle said aloud.

Stickle was in the woods, so he felt that he could grant permission to himself to speak out loud. Eggplant Charlie used to do the same thing in his healthier days. He would go into the woods and start talking to himself. Talking to oneself is not crazy or even eccentric because everyone does it, but it is considered anti-social. Talking to yourself on the bus is one way to ensure your own private seat. Talking to oneself while walking down a city street used to be considered a sign of schizophrenia, but with the advent of hands-free cell phones, that behavior is considered more acceptable, or at least less pathological than it was in the recent past.

Talking aloud to oneself is clearly not the same thing as thinking silently to oneself. For one thing, the speaker is clearly using words. The speaker is also listening. In a sense, the speaker is having a conversation with himself or herself. However, even though the speaker and the listener inhabit the same body, are they really the same? When a person engages in this extremely private form of conversation, maybe that person is trying to resolve some kind of inner conflict by having the warring parties parley.

Another function of talking to oneself is language acquisition. When toddlers babble or imitate bits of adult conversation while playing alone, they are practicing speech. Talking to oneself is useful to adults, as well, when they are trying to learn a second language or if they are rehearsing a speech in their first.

Eggplant Charlie used to walk alone in the woods to "get himself together" before a busy market day or a visit to a public place. He needed to reconcile the misanthropic side of himself with the part of himself that needed to do business with his fellow *Homo sapiens*. He did not go into the woods with the explicit purpose of talking to himself, but the words would just spill out. The sights and smells and feels of the forest energized him as he would subconsciously prepare himself for dealings with the public. *"That'll be six dollars. Do you have anything smaller? The muscatines will be ready next week, and I know your old lady is gonna want some to make jam. You can make wine from' em too, you know."* And so on.

When Stickle walked through the woods, he felt a tremendous sense of relief. While he was drawing breath, the woods provided great refuge for a drinking man. In addition to being able to take a decent pull from a bottle beyond the field of vision of temperance busybodies, he could chat with himself and sing bits of the songs he was composing.

After Stickle died, he still took pleasure in walking in the woods. Being invisible, he no longer had to worry about people watching him drink. If he were so inclined, he could bring a jug of whiskey to a Southern Baptist sermon and swig from it in front of the choir, and no one would be the wiser, but Stickle had no desire to flaunt his alcoholism or, in any way, show disrespect toward people who were earnestly trying to find their way by attending religious services. The pleasure came from being able to speak aloud to himself without causing the living to feel that they were "hearing things", or even worse "hearing voices." Righteous ghosts are careful to avoid speaking to, or around, the living. Demons, of course, take great pleasure in doing so.

Stickle also used the woods for language acquisition. He would practice various squirrel tongues, and bird dialects. He didn't much care if animals or birds heard him. He figured he was doing no harm.

When Stickle uttered these words in nineteenth-century Mid-Atlantic American English—"What a foul spirit I am! I need a drink"—he was creating a situation similar to that described in the old Zen koan, "If a tree falls in the forest, and if nobody is there to hear it, does it make a noise?" Well, if a "ghost" speaks out loud in the woods behind the State Line Veterinarians building, and nobody can hear him but a bunch of squirrels, does it make any difference?

Before you answer, you should be warned about something. If you were an apprentice to a Zen master, and you tried to answer this question, the master would hit you over the head in order to emphasize the ultimate futility of words, and perhaps spark a nanosecond- long moment of enlightenment in you. There are many dropouts from these kinds of training programs because these lessons seem to be lacking something in the pedagogy department. However, in all fairness, others seem satisfied. Whether or not they actually achieve the "aha" moment known as *satori* is debatable, prompting another koan-like question: If an apprentice to a Zen master keeps his mouth shut after being asked one of these rhetorical questions, does that mean that he has been enlightened, or does that mean that he has recognized the fact that this is a rhetorical question that does not require an answer, or does it mean that he doesn't want to get hit again, or does it mean something else?

In the case of Stickle's audible utterance in the ostensibly audience-free woods behind the vet's office, it meant something else.

The tree falls. It makes a noise. The birds hear it. The cicadas sense it. The earthworms and ants record it as a catastrophic event. *Nobody* rarely really means *nobody*, especially in the forest.

Stickle took his flask out of his stinky jacket and uncorked it. In the three-dimensional world that Sam and Eggplant Charlie called home one can say that a flask typically contains distilled *spirits*. In Stickle's realm, the flask contained *a* distilled *spirit, a spirit* being a singular entity, or distilled *spirit, spirit* without the indefinite article indicating an uncountable substance, but not distilled *spirits, spirits* with a final *–s* which means *spirits* is in a plural form which would entail their being separable entities with boundaries.

You know what happens when one uncorks a flask or bottle or other vessel containing *a spirit.* The spirit is released, and it expresses gratitude. In various myths, it grants its liberator a wish, or two, or three. In a 1960's sitcom, the spirit was a beautiful woman who served as an astronaut's live-in female companion.

Well, all that is legend, which means that it has a kernel of truth to it.

Stickle had been left to roam the world, to do good after he died as a result of his own stupidity, leaving a grieving but, frankly, somewhat relieved widow and a couple of orphans who hadn't seen him for months, anyway. He had been allowed to keep his attachment to alcohol, which he figured he would need in order to get his work done as he had when he was three dimensional.

Stickle hadn't been a stupid man and he hadn't become a stupid "ghost", but he was capable of doing stupid things. Alcohol was frequently described as a demon in his human times, and his own struggle with this perceived demon was reflected in the lyrics he penned while he was drawing breath.

> *Toast me not friends*
>
> *And lift no stein*
>
> *For the glory is*
>
> *Not rightly mine*
>
> *While you are good,*
>
> *And good to see*
>
> *Toast me not friends*
>
> *And leave me be.*

That tune, like all of Stickle's tunes, was catchy and had a way of persuading the gate-keepers of the listeners' long-term memories to let it enter among the other timeless tunes that make up the trans-generational soundtrack of American culture.

He sang it now, as he uncorked his flask while sitting on a pile of aromatic pine needles. The squirrels were chattering and rolling away next to him, oblivious to his presence.

The spirit exited the bottle as a misty cloud, in a way that would have been familiar to Eggplant Charlie, who had grown up watching the 1960's sitcom about the astronaut and the genie.

This form was also familiar to Stephen Ray Stickle, who, while drawing breath, had a mystical streak and a taste for the exotic, so he had read all the stories from Araby about *djinn,* or genies, and their magical wish granting abilities.

Stickle was a little upset by this visitation, however. He wasn't panicky, but it distressed him that alcohol-induced hallucinations, or d.t.s, would follow him into the afterlife. This one wasn't bad, but would he experience the ones with which he had become familiar in the realm or mortals and immortals? He remembered being covered with cockroaches in a hotel room in North Carolina and shrugging it off as a hallucination. One of his roommates—in those days a hotel guest shared a room and a bed with strangers—screamed when he saw Stickle on the floor because he thought Stickle had died. Stickle had *really* been covered with cockroaches and had been too befuddled by demon alcohol to brush them off. Why brush off figments of your imagination?

That identical thought occurred to Eggplant Charlie after the doctor had left. He assessed his situation. He was incapacitated, but apparently out of the woods, in a manner of speaking. He also seemed to be out of his mind, but he needed to get something done. He needed to get out of here, go find Cauliflower, and get back to his life. He had looked death in the face and decided that he didn't much mind dying, but Cauliflower needed him, and that was an important reason to keep on keeping on.

Out of the blue, the thought dawned on him, the thought inadvertently sent telepathically to no one in particular by the only being who seemed to possess a bona fide claim to being real to Eggplant Charlie over the past… what? …two days?… three days? Anyway, he got it. Eggplant Charlie was an eligible receiver of a clumsily thrown notion tossed out by the fumbling, stumbling quarterback of notions, the late great Stephen Ray Stickle.

"Why brush off figments of your imagination?"

The doctor was a part of him, a pretty female part of him at that. Did that mean that she couldn't help? Why not? After this was over, maybe Dr. Barbie/Eggplant Charlie could get together with Miss America/Mark Metacomet over a drink at the Old Post Road Inn and talk about old times. Just us girls--ladies' night out. Eggplant Charlie fumbled for his bedpan and puked. Maybe with a cleaned-out body, his mind might start functioning properly again.

The fog didn't take the form of the astronaut's blonde girlfriend, which didn't surprise Stickle since he had died a hundred years before the first episode of that sitcom aired, and he wouldn't have gotten the reference. It looked like a cloud, basically, with a human visage including approximations of eyes, a nose and a mouth.

"Hello, my friend. Do I get three wishes?" asked Stickle.

"How about me, friend. Do I get one?" asked the *djinn*.

"Well, I suppose turnabout is fair play. I'm pretty limited when it comes to wish granting powers, though," responded Stickle.

"It's a modest one, friend."

"Well, what will it be then, then? I'm all ears. I got nothing else, I guess," said Stickle.

"I only ask that you not imbibe me right away. I've known you about as well, and about as intimately, as I've known anybody, and I'd like to speak with you, as one being to another, without being immediately assimilated into your bloodstream."

"Fair enough," said Stickle. "I suppose you aren't real, unlike those Carolina cockroaches. I guess you are just another vision of hell. I thought I had gotten shed of those visions and sensations when I stopped drawing breath."

"You're a funny man, Stickle. You're a 'ghost' asking a 'demon' if he is real or not. You see any irony in that whatsoever, or are your brains entirely pickled?'

Stickle laughed. He saw the irony, all right. He also thought that he was laughing at his own joke since he thought the *djinn* was a part of him, or at least a figment of his imagination.

"I reckon they are floating around the celestial void in a big barrel filled with gin," he replied, this time really laughing at his own joke even though it wasn't all that funny. Puns usually aren't, and this one, involving the words *gin* and *djinn*, was more a groaner than a knee-slapper. Stickle was just trying to be sociable, even if he was just socializing with himself.

The *djinn* laughed too, which bothered Stickle a little. Who needs two aspects of the same person to be laughing at the same joke? The *djinn* saw that Stickle had stopped laughing, and he abruptly stopped as well, and then he spoke as though he could read Stickle's mind, which he really couldn't.

"I'm not you, sir. This is a mistake you have made in the past, and one you keep on making. I was hoping that you would see the light after you died, but you never have. I'm not you, and you're not me. Please stop identifying yourself with me," warned the *djinn*.

"Well, introduce yourself then, sir, for at present, you seem to have me at a disadvantage. You clearly know who I am, and I thought I knew who you were, but I am plainly wrong, as you seem to be correcting me."

"You know me well. You've written songs about me. You've cursed me. You've loved me. You've spent your last penny on me. You've neglected your family so that you could spend more time with me. You've attributed your brilliance and your creativity to me, and you've used me as a scapegoat for your periods of inactivity and idleness. You know who I am, but you don't see that I'm not really who you are. You think you love me, and you think you need me, but you don't," said the *djinn*.

"All right, sir. Since you won't be straightforward with me and would prefer to ask me to solve riddles like some kind of foggy sphinx, I'll make an educated guess and call you Demon Alcohol," said Stickle.

"And you'd be wrong again. Think about that label *demon*. There, but for the grace of heaven, go you, my friend. Answer this one for me---what good is alcohol?"

"Aw, no good, I guess," replied Stickle.

"Come on. You know better. No good?"

"Well, you can put it on wounds, like those on the back of a whipped slave, and it'll keep the wound from festering," ventured Stickle.

"And?" coaxed the *djinn*.

"I helped out in Washington in the early days of the war. I helped with the wounded, but I had no stomach for it and left after a couple of days."

"And?"

"They'd have to saw the arms and legs off these boys they brought in, both Federal and secessionist—just young boys. Anyway, they didn't have much laudanum on hand, but they had plenty of whisky."

"And?"

"They gave them whisky before they started sawing off their limbs."

"And?"

"It didn't kill the pain, but it made it easier to bear."

"You only stayed for a couple of days. Why?" asked the *djinn*.

"I wasn't much good at anything by then. I was a drunk."

"Wrong! Try again. Why?"

"The pain was too much."

"How did you deal with it?"

"I took you into my system."

"I didn't help you much, though, did I?"

"No. I couldn't stay. There was a crazy fellow with a long beard from Jersey who was really good at it, though."

"Really good at what?"

"Helping the boys."

"Helping the boys do what?"

Stickle had thought about this question before, and now, for the first time in over a hundred and forty years, he was able to answer.

"Helping the boys die. I wasn't any good at that. I was a drunken crybaby, but crazy old Walt Whitman had a gift for it."

"That wasn't your mission while you were drawing breath, so you weren't any good at it. You didn't leave because of me, so don't you curse me for it," scolded the *djinn*. "Walt Whitman was designed for it."

"Where is he now?" inquired Stickle.

"He was released from the cycle of rebirth, but when a being has that kind of talent, paradise just seems like a shelf in a root cellar. He volunteered to go back."

"Where's he at?"

"No place you'd recognize friend, but I guarantee it makes those field hospitals in Washington look like luxury hotels."

"How about you? Are you a demon?"

"I'm not an angel. I'm not a Buddha. I'm a spirit; I'm a substance. I can cleanse the wounds of a whipped slave or ease the pain of surgery. I can also shrink a liver so that it won't function any more. I can make an inn a place of warmth and fellowship or turn it into a riotous scene of murder. It's all me, and none of it is me. I'm a substance."

"You're not a demon?"

"Mister Stickle, you make me laugh. You're a ghost? You're not a ghost? You are a funny being. What is a demon? What does a demon do? You tell me. How would you define a demon?"

"A demon torments souls. It is a malicious spirit," said Stickle.

"Have I tormented you?"

"Yes!"

"Wrong! Am I a malicious spirit?"

"Why did you make me abandon my family?" asked Stickle.

"I never made you do anything, Stickle. I'm not like you and that squirrel or that grouchy farmer. I am a substance. I sting; I cleanse. I can be used as a poison or a medicine. Folks use me: I don't use them."

"You've tormented me!"

"You have tormented yourself by telling yourself that you needed me, and that you couldn't compose music without me. You also tormented yourself by telling yourself that you hated me. When you tell yourself that you hate or love someone or something and that you cannot live with or without that someone or something, then you are demonizing them. You can demonize anybody or anything, just by attaching yourself to her or him or it."

"So why can't I break this attachment? I've tried. I've sworn you off," asked Stickle.

"That's like saying to a lover, 'I can never see you again. I hereby break my attachment to you.' You'll be more attached than ever to that lover whether you see her again or not. Breaking an attachment is not an illocutionary act like making or breaking a promise. You can only break an attachment by looking at whatever or whomever you are attached to and seeing her, him or it for what he she or it really is. Look at me. What do you see?"

"A cloud with a face."

"Fair enough, and that's not who I really am. What I mean is…"

"I know. I'm not stupid. I am very weak, though. How can I deal with the pain of being dead and with the fact that I made a mess of my life when I was drawing breath and that I hurt those whom I loved the most? How can I do that without you?"

"Those things don't need to be dealt with, Stephen."

The spirit was using his first name now, a detail which was not unnoticed by Stickle.

"They just *are*. They just *have been*. They are simply facts. They are like me. They are not malicious, and they are not charitable. They just *are*. Abhor them; take delight in them; it doesn't matter. They just *are*, like me. Let us *be*," added the *djinn*.

"That's a tall order."

"It's not an order. It's just counsel that I offer in the spirit of friendship, and I'd like for us to recognize each other as friends."

"Okay then, friend," said Stickle. "I've certainly thought of you as a friend before, so I guess I can again. Tell me again about Walt Whitman. How could he do that of which I was incapable? How could he help young soldiers die? Where did that strength come from? Was it just because he was such an odd duck?

"He knew what you know now. How can you really love someone and be attached? The dying soldiers needed his help, and he gave it because he did not let attachment to their prognosis or to the color of their uniforms distract him from his mission. His emotions welled up at times, and he wept, but he wasn't afraid of his emotions or his own tears. They were there, but he did not try to deal with them. He let them *be*."

"**A**w, let her be, Lilith! What the hell! Poor woman's in jail or somewhere now."

"That's where she belongs! She damn near killed him! If she ever gets out on parole, I hope you're not gonna let her work here again!"

Managing the co-op was a relatively difficult gig. There wasn't much money in it, and, for all the counter-culture virtues it exemplified, the career choice, if you could call it that, sometimes stirred feelings of regret in Dan.--just plain Dan, one syllable and a short form of the name his parents had given him, Daniel Jackson. He had no noble blood, no Indian blood, and no claim to having supernatural powers. Dan was a down-to- earth earth hippie. Friends of his had chosen other lifestyles, and Dan had gotten glimpses of them. He was sometimes invited to spend weekends on yachts and vacation homes, and he usually accepted these invitations. Why not? He was happy enough with decision to pursue his "alternative" lifestyle. There wasn't much in the way of cash rewards, but there was the feeling that he had somehow avoided the rat race.

At times like these, however, when a volunteer seemed particularly rat-like, he felt no freer than a data entry clerk in a maze of office cubicles. Why couldn't the co-op people simply be nice to each other? What does co-op mean, anyhow? How come Lilith was still trashing Cauliflower? Why kick a person when that person is down? Dan really couldn't fire Lilith for being a bitch. There was a procedure for firing people, but it had never been used. People left of their own free will; they got angry or sick of working for produce and discounts instead of money and quit, but nobody had ever been fired.

How does that procedure work? thought Dan. Well, he couldn't remember, but it involved one verbal warning, one written warning, a probation period, and then, if all the parties involved were still alive, termination. Dan had never really given Lilith any formal verbal warnings. He had informally admonished her many a time, but never followed up with a threatened consequence. After the admonitions, Lilith would always smile a little malicious smile and go back to shelving cans or something. To Dan, that smile always seemed to say, "*Whatever, little man. I can crush you like a bug whenever I want.*"

Dan had had one disastrous date with Lilith once upon a long time ago. To make a long story short, she had let him know that what she had planned for the evening involved costumes, role-play, and props that were way too halloweeny for one-syllable Dan. *Oh! Damn! No, thank you ma'am.*

That was a long time ago, and different strokes for different folks and all that, but this time, Lilith had really gotten to old Dan. He really liked Eggplant Charlie and he really missed Cauliflower's presence at the co-op. He had been at The Old Post Inn for Mark Metacomet's shameful performance, and he had walked out on it before Mark Metacomet's dramatic exit.

Lilith gave him one of her nasty post-scolding smiles, and this time, Dan decided to let her have it, dominatrix or no dominatrix, Dan was a man, damn it, not a mouse.

"You know, Lilith, if Cauliflower walked through that door right now, covered in blood, I'd give her her old job back, no questions asked, and if you decided to seek employment elsewhere, I really wouldn't care a bit."

Lilith didn't smile. She glared at Dan, took her green employee's apron off and threw it, and walked off the job. Dan felt kind of remorseful. She was reasonably diligent, and it could be said that she added a little spice to the blandness of the life of the manager of the natural foods co-op. Halloween has its place, after all, as long as every day isn't Halloween.

Jail works on smart people, and Mark Metacomet was relatively smart. Jail doesn't work on the less intelligent among us because they often lack the ability to make cognitive connections between cause and effect. When relatively smart people are put in a dirty cell with a dirty bunk on which to sit and a dirty toilet in which to urinate and defecate in full view of everyone, they quickly realize that jail is a bad place to be. They want to leave jail as soon as possible, but they can't. They must wait. There are no magazines to read, nor is there a television or stimulating conversation. There is nothing to do but think about the situation. The relatively intelligent people who find themselves in jail due to a lapse in their relative intelligence usually realize that they are at least partly, if not completely to blame for the revocation of their freedom. As the time slowly passes, they reconstruct the events which led them to their unfortunate circumstances and puzzle out ways to prevent similar sequences of events from leading to similar outcomes.

The less intelligent yell and scream a lot and refuse to sit still and curse, and so on. The police and the jailers say things like, "We can make this easy, or we can make this hard," and given this choice, the less intelligent often choose the latter.

Mark Metacomet wanted to make it as easy as possible so that the time would pass as quickly as possible. He did not want to have a lot of interesting stories to tell after his release.

The charges were public drunkenness, disturbing the peace, and indecent exposure. Mark Metacomet felt that he was technically innocent of all of these charges, but he also felt that he had recently done some things which, while technically weren't illegal, were, nonetheless, despicable.

"I'm guilty of making Cauliflower pissed off at Eggplant Charlie by singing that stupid song, so she tried to bite him to death," he said aloud to himself. He was alone, or so he thought, so his talking aloud would not be interpreted as a sign of derangement, but his analysis lacked credibility. Why?

"A stupid song is just a stupid song. Cauliflower forgot about it after a couple of weeks. Okay, Eggplant Charlie was still sore, but so what? Why am I in jail? I'm guilty of singing another stupid song about Cauliflower's viral video. So what? I'm a troubadour. I report the news; I don't create it."

It was true. Singing a nasty song was no offense for which a person should be jailed.

"Okay. I'm guilty of exploiting Eggplant Charlie's misfortune and Cauliflower's running amok for personal gain. That was wrong. I shouldn't have done it.

Okay, but it still didn't warrant incarceration.

"I'm guilty of planning to use Lilith to satisfy my carnal desires even though I had no intention of pursuing a meaningful relationship or even a friendship with her."

He did say that, but only because he had a lot of time on his hands. Lilith was a man-eater, and he couldn't have hurt her with a bulldozer. He was not guilty of anything there but recklessness, of thinking that he could come out of a dalliance with Lilith unscathed even though no other male he knew had been able to pull that off.

"I'm guilty of seeing something that wasn't there. Why the hell did I see a giant...what? A giant mouse like a field mouse, not even a rat, the size of a bear."

Not guilty by reason of insanity. Temporary insanity? What had caused him to see a walking, talking mouse in the men's room of The Old Post Road Inn? Was it a human in a mouse costume? No, absolutely not. It was definitely a mouse.

"I'm guilty of running down the street with my genitals exposed."

Yes, indeed, and that is not acceptable behavior. Jumbo must stay in his cage.

"I'm guilty of public drunkenness."

No. he hadn't had that much to drink, and the shock of seeing the big mouse eliminated any possible effect the alcohol could have had.

"I'm guilty of disturbing the peace."

No. That's just a bullshit charge cops lay on you when they dislike you.

"I really don't deserve to be here at all," Mark Metacomet finally decided.

"In the realm of mortals and immortals, your reality, that is, people do not get what they deserve. They are tried and tested. Your just desserts come later. Believe me, I know."

Mark Metacomet could hear the voice and smell the b.o. and gin, but he couldn't see anybody. As far as he could *see*, he had the jail to himself, which, up until now, he had counted as a small blessing. Jail isn't a place where one really wants company if one can avoid it.

The voice sounded familiar. It did not sound like it was coming from inside him. It felt, smelt and sounded as if another human were with him in the cell, but it sure didn't look like it.

"Hello? Anyone here?"

"You're here, ain't you?" Stickle couldn't help himself. He knew Mark Metacomet's soul was in danger and that he needed and deserved help, but he simply didn't like this man very much. Stickle rarely used the word *ain't* outside of his songs, but when he was trifling with someone, it would emerge as kind of a code word.

"Am I nuts? You sound like the talking mouse. Was it real? Are you real?"

"Well, let's see. The answer to your first question is 'maybe', because I'm a poor judge of these things. The answer to your second question is, 'after a fashion', and the answer to your third question is 'yes, definitely', although sometimes I have trouble manifesting myself in your realm."

"Are you the mouse?" asked Metacomet.

"I've just gotten a stern lecture from Alcohol, who doesn't want to be called 'Demon Alcohol' anymore, about the folly of identifying myself with this and that, so the question you just asked is disagreeable to me, and I respectfully decline to answer."

"You asked me the same question, you bastard," observed Mark Metacomet.

"No, not really. I said, 'Are you *a* man or *a* mouse?' There was no definite article in my question, only the indefinite *a* meaning any undifferentiated mouse. I did not ask, 'Are you *the* mouse', because using *the* would have indicated a specific mouse that I had either mentioned before or one with which we were both familiar and to which I was obviously referring. I also used the word *or*, which, when used in a yes/no question is a way of asking two questions. I was asking you these two questions, Mark Metacomet. First, are you a male human who subscribes to the tacit code of behavior shared by the males in this culture? That question actually entails these questions as well. Are you manly? Do you aspire to manliness? Are you brave? Can you take risks? Are you willing to sacrifice immediate gratification for the higher principles of honesty, fidelity and friendship?"

Stickle continued, "My second question is, are you a non-subscriber to this cultural code—a metaphorical mouse? This question entails several others as well. Are you cowardly? Are you willing to have your friends slandered and insulted and even participate in the slanderous process simply to get some instant gratification? Simply to get, as Mister Bones might say in the minstrel line, your hambone boiled?"

"Okay. I know you're not coming from inside me because I don't think like that, and I sure don't talk like that. Where are you coming from?" asked Mark Metacomet.

"I was born in Orwigsburg, Pennsylvania, but I've been all over. I'm no stranger to The Old Post Road Inn."

"So you're Edgar Allan Poe?"

"Do I talk like Edgar Allan Poe?"

"I don't know. I've never met the guy. Have you?"

"Yes. He had a good voice. He'd sing along with my songs sometimes. He wasn't what you'd call a jolly good fellow, though. One minute he'd be entertaining folks with his stories, and the next he'd be nursing a drink off in the corner by himself. Anyway, I've met him, sure, but I can't say I really know him."

"So you're a ghost?"

"I don't like that word. It makes me sound evil or something. I died in your realm, but I can still visit here with my memories and ego intact, so, if you have to pin a label on me, I guess you can call me a 'ghost'."

"Can anyone else hear you?"

"Everyone else can hear me. Most people don't listen to me. Right now, we seem to be alone. I'd shut up if someone else were to come into the room. I'd hate to see you locked up permanently, so it won't do to have you talking to folks who aren't there using different voices."

"Who are you? I'm Mark Metacomet. I'm a direct descendant of King Phillip. You know me. You know that. Who are you, besides not being Edgar Allan Poe?"

"Stephen Ray Stickle."

"Eggplant Charlie's favorite. That figures."

"We are bound together by mystic chords of memory and even sturdier twine."

"That's great. Can you get me out of here?"

"Has this experience helped you? Have you learned from it?' asked Stickle.

"Does your answer depend on my answer?"

"Yes."

"Then yes."

"Good. Listen. Act sane. Let `em know you had a bad scare while you were sleepwalking. You fell asleep at the bar and you were still sleeping while you were screaming and giving your manhood some fresh air.

"That'll work?"

"Yeah. Admit to something. Disturbing the peace is no big thing. Admit to that."

"Okay, and they won't call me a sex offender and send me away if I do that?" asked Mark Metacomet.

"No, they won't. Now, I want you to do something in exchange. You might think it's for me, but it's not. You might think it's for Eggplant Charlie or Cauliflower, but it's not. It's for you. Right now, you have virtually no chance of escaping the endless cycle of rebirth, and you might not even get to be a human being next time. You've got to clean up your hand, friend. You've got to do some good, and it wouldn't hurt if you got Lilith to help you."

"Lilith? Fat chance. She thinks I'm a lunatic."

"She thinks you're a jerk, but so what? She's right. Furthermore, you think she's a bitch. Now, I don't care for that word, but I need to speak plainly. She is a bitch; you're right. So what? Save each other! Untie this double noose that you have tied together before you hang yourselves together with it."

"What do you want me to do? Marry her?" asked Mark Metacomet.

Stickle laughed at that idea. "You two need to set Cauliflower free and restore her reputation. Eggplant Charlie doesn't know this, and I'm not allowed to tell him, but he may be at death's door. If he stops drawing breath, he'll feel compelled to stick around as what you call a 'ghost' to look after Cauliflower, and he'll most likely do more harm than good and get himself caught between dimensions with a boatload of attachments. Do you want that for your friend?"

"No, I don't guess I do," said Mark Metacomet. "What should I do?"

"I can't micromanage things for you. You move through this realm with much greater ease than I do. You're intelligent. Please figure it out. I have to go. This is exhausting."

Mark Metacomet sat back on the bunk and thought, out loud, again.

"What have I done to deserve this?"

Stickle heard these words as he left, still invisible to most of those in Metacomet's dimension. They made him wince. He was tired. Persuading humans was not much easier than influencing squirrels at times. He reached for the flask in his coat pocket and sat down on the bench outside the courthouse across the street from the police station where Mark Metacomet's holding cell was located.. He wasn't particularly thirsty right then. He uncorked the flask, but he didn't take a nip. No *djinn* escaped from the bottle this time. He brought the neck of the flask to his nostrils and sniffed--smelled like gin. He poured a little out on the sidewalk--looked like gin. How could there be gin in this dimension? How could he drink, for that matter? In the one hundred and fifty odd years it had been since he had died, he hadn't eaten a thing, but he continued to drink like a fish. How come he never had to pee? While he was drawing breath, he constantly had to pee.

He thought back to one of the first things he remembered hearing from another ` ghost' after he had been initiated into the ethereal fraternity of apparitions. It was this false paradox: *"Ghosts can smell, but they can't smell."* It was a stupid pun, but it was true. `Ghosts" can *smell* in the stative sense in that people can sometimes smell them. `Ghosts' are not supposed to retain their olfactory ability after they cease drawing breath, so they can't *smell* in the active sense, so how come Stickle could smell the gin in his flask?

"This stuff can't be the same stuff I drank when I was alive," he mused quietly, but aloud. What was it then? Was it still alcohol? Who or what was alcohol anyway?

Demons, contrary to conventional wisdom, are not always malignant, sadistic beings from hell. Sometimes they are fumbling, good- natured ghosts who have crossed the line one too many times, and who have somehow, accidentally, ended up in the tormenting business. Even the demon who had masqueraded as Miss America and Mark Metacomet and who had been exposed by Eggplant Charlie had given the grouchy farmer some decent advice, which was that Eggplant Charlie's misanthropy wasn't logical or helpful.

Demons often have a remorseful nature. They know that they are in trouble with the powers that be and that they are in violation of the laws governing the universe. Sometimes they try to warn those who seem to following the path they have taken themselves into demonhood and misery.

Alcohol is not a demon, but the attachment to alcohol is. The substance known as alcohol really existed only in the realm of mortals and immortals and not in Stickle's dimension. The stuff in Stickle's flask was not alcohol *per se*, it was, in fact, the essence of attachment. If he poured it out, it would just refill itself because renunciation only reinforces attachment.

If he "drank" it, he would take it inside himself and renew his commitment and attachment to it. This stuff had caused him problems in the past, and it was confusing him now. How can one break an attachment? It was like breaking liquid, and this attachment was in liquid form.

"*I can't deal with this now, I'll just let it be,*" he thought, almost silently. He corked the flask and put it back in his stinky coat.

"I wonder how those silly squirrels are getting along," he said aloud, carelessly causing the old man sitting next to him to look around for a man who might be talking to him. Stickle headed out for the vet's office on the state line. *"If the squirrels get it, they get it. If they don't, they don't. I've got my own problems,"* he thought.

Cauliflower was powering up. The drugs were not affecting her much anymore because a part of her brain had figured out what made them work and sent a signal to her glands to release just the right amount of stuff to counteract them.

Eggplant Charlie wasn't doing as well. His wounds had become infected, and since the doctors didn't know he had been bitten by a squirrel, they didn't test him for a certain virus which is only transmitted by squirrel bite, one which mimicked the symptoms of head trauma and which could be fatal if left untreated.

Eggplant Charlie fell asleep and dreamed, not of the minstrel line, not of *Star Trek,* and not of pretty actresses or doctors. Eggplant Charlie dreamed about flying—The Flying Dream. It was his favorite. It was blissful. He was floating in air as if the air were water. He pushed himself off walls and buildings and trees as if they were the walls of swimming pools.

The dream started off with walking. Then, gravity seemed to be reduced so that the steps were bounds like those of the astronauts on the moon. Finally, gravity became so diminished that a little push off a tree could send a person fifteen miles. It was a very sweet dream. The dream could last forever if not for...... Cauliflower!

Eggplant Charlie's eyes opened. He could tell he had a high fever, and he knew that he might not be long for this dimension. What would become of Cauliflower?

Mark Metacomet's audience with the judge took all of about five minutes. He had spent the night in jail. He hadn't caused any trouble, having decided to "do it the easy way." He took Stickle's advice about using somnambulism as an excuse. He had had no priors involving indecent exposure, and the judge hadn't seen the viral you tube video, so he figured the guy just forgot to zip up. Mark was fined five hundred dollars for disturbing the peace, which was about half of his life's savings at that point, and more than what he usually made in a week as a laborer and a musician. Nevertheless, he had it, so he paid it. Now that he was free, he had a mission to complete, and, although he didn't have a clear plan, he knew where to start. He needed to talk with Lilith.

Stickle contemplated Sam. Sam's preachy chattering had ceased. The other squirrels had ignored him, and he felt he wasn't doing much good by chattering about stuff which he really didn't understand himself.

Sam didn't understand what was wrong with himself because he didn't have much of a long-term memory, but his real problem was homesickness. None of the squirrels in these woods understood him. Sam's home was only about a mile and a half away, which doesn't seem like much to a human being, but that is a mile and a half of cats and dogs, criss-crossed by asphalt death traps with cars and trucks barreling down them.

Even if Stickle could have shown Sam the way home, the odds were that he would never make it. The good news was that Sam's sense of balance was recovering, and he was beginning to jump in the canopy of pines as he had done in the canopy of sweet gums and swamp maples before his encounter with Eggplant Charlie. The jumps were slow and clumsy at first because Sam was hedging his bets as he leapt from skinny branch to skinny branch, but then something in his brain became reactivated. It is what every squirrel and downhill skier comes to realize. The more one tries to be in control, the more likely it is for that someone to fall. When a novice skier says, "Whoa, now, that's too fast!", he or she will sure enough end up on the ground. When a squirrel thinks that the branch is just a little too far away a nanosecond before leaping to the next branch, he or she won't make it either. Well, Sam had been grounded, and, as delightful as accumulated pine needles are, they are no match for leaping, so he overcame his lack of self- confidence and started taking bolder and bolder leaps until he was almost the squirrel he once was, jumping in the treetops and feeling the words *rolling in special dirt* as he leapt.

Metaphorically speaking, Bones was a chameleon. As a surgeon, back in Stickle's day, in the realm of mortals and immortals, he was "white", when he was in Eggplant Charlie's minstrel line, he was "black". A chameleon, or a flounder, for that matter, uses its regular sensory organs to send messages about its environment to the pigment-containing chromatophores in its skin, and so it is able to blend in with its environment. Bones used his hunches about what human beings were thinking to activate structures in his makeup that were analogous to chromatophores in certain cold blooded creatures in order to achieve a sort of camouflage. Thus, to Eggplant Charlie, he was black. Being black during the time of Eggplant Charlie's hospitalization would allow Bones to be part of the minstrel line and be a medical professional at the same time.

That trick wouldn't have worked so well in the 1960's when Bones was the chief medical officer about a starship in a "fictional" television series. America was ready for a black communications officer at that point, a position which seemed to be the inter-galactic equivalent of a telephone operator, but a surgeon? Maybe, but it probably would have proved even more distracting than the communication officer's mini-skirt.

Even when Bones was drawing breath, he never paid much conscious attention to his own physical appearance, and after his demise, he quit caring much about the dimension he was in. He had made the transition from being a "real" Civil War surgeon in the realm of mortals and immortals to being a "fictional" character in a 1960's science fiction series relatively seamlessly. His ego was giving him some grief about his latest role in Eggplant Charlie's "hallucinatory" minstrel show, however. The one constant throughout his existence was being called "Bones". However, it bothered him, when he was part of the minstrel line, along with Mr. Interlocutor and Eggplant Charlie (a.k.a.

Mr. Tambo), to be referred to as "*Mister* Bones." He was a *doctor*, damn it!

Bones had always been attached to anger, but from where did that anger emanate? Why did he despise Vulcans so much? Why was he so hard on Mr. Tambo?

Bones was *angry*, but it might be more accurate to say that Bones was *anger*. Bones was a demon, but he was bad at it, just as he was bad at being a righteous ghost. He wasn't much at tormenting people because he was too disgusted with people to want much to do with them either way.

Oddly enough, during the Civil War, he had been good at fixing them. This was because he wasn't angry with the maimed soldiers who were sent his way. He was angry with those who had sent them.

Bones was two-faced. He was anger and he was righteous anger. Anger, of course, is a deadly sin, and righteous anger is, well, righteous. No one looks back at Jesus's driving the moneychangers out of the temple and says, "Tsk, tsk. He should have had a better handle on his emotions." All this means that Bones could never be properly sorted into one of the classifications in the binary system of good and evil.

Bones didn't care much at all about violating the laws of the universe when he was a righteous ghost. He would transmogrify himself whenever it suited him, just to piss people off. When people formed attachments to him, he was delighted, not dismayed as he was supposed to be, and utterances such as, "I hate you! I hope I never see you again!" were music to his ears.

Therefore, they made him a demon, but his heart wasn't into that, either. He was always trying to fix people up, especially their bodies, so he was a failure as a tormentor.

Bones' original nickname was *Sawbones*. That's an interesting word. It's an English compound noun formed like a Spanish compound noun with a verb spliced on to a noun like *matasanos*, the Spanish word for *quack*. If it were translated so that it worked like *sawbones,* it would be *killhealthyfolks*. A similar example is the word *chupacabra,* which would be *suckgoat*. That is the name of a legendary vampire creature which lives in Puerto Rico and mutilates livestock.

Bones sawed plenty of bones during the Civil War, more in a week than an average surgeon did over a lifetime. He suffered from what we would call post- traumatic stress disorder from hearing soldiers scream as he inflicted unspeakable pain on them in an effort to save their lives. All the while, he grew angrier and angrier at the people who had sent a generation of young Americans into raging storms of lead.

Bones was creeped out by Walt Whitman, but he recognized the fact that his services were needed. Stephen Ray Stickle was more to his liking. Bones liked drunks, especially when they got angry. However, he was not disappointed when Stickle decided he could no longer volunteer under the conditions which existed in the field hospital. That seemed to be a perfectly rational choice to Bones, and their friendship continued into the afterlife. Righteous ghosts and demons aren't really supposed to maintain friendships, but the bonds forged under certain conditions, such as those that existed in the field hospitals, are not easily broken, not even by heaven.

After his descent into demonhood, Bones hung out at hospitals a lot, where he was supposed to torment the patients, both righteous and ungodly, in order to either test them or help them pay their karmic bills, but Bones couldn't resist being a doctor, and he frequently gave more effective treatments and better advice than did the real doctors.

No one knew what to do with Bones. He could not be returned to the cycle of rebirth, not after he had been a demon. If he were allowed to be a righteous ghost again, it would make a mockery of all the rules and set a catastrophic precedent, so the powers that be made a special adjudication regarding Bones, "Let him *be!*"

And so he *was*.

Bones made an attempt to look in on Cauliflower, but the second he opened the door, he was blinded by her pure light, so he closed the door immediately. He saw spots in front of his eyes for about fifteen minutes.

Eggplant Charlie, in contrast, was a perfect candidate for the kind of torment offered up by Bones. Eggplant Charlie knew anger quite well, both the righteous and ungodly varieties. He thought he had learned to master it, but demons do not serve human masters. Anger is a demon best managed by both observing it and ignoring it, depending on the situation. A person should observe it when it attempts to take possession of that person, and ignore it, when it has taken possession of another. Anger is a goading demon, one which baits its trap with the stinky cheese of revenge. All this sage advice had never been applied by Eggplant Charlie, who used to display explosive anger, which, over the years, had mellowed into a kind of simmering anger that seemed to be always present, except, of course, when Cauliflower was around.

The advice offered in The Good Book to turn the other cheek when struck is truly demon bane. Forgiveness is also powerful medicine. Unfortunately, Eggplant Charlie was not long on forgiveness, and as for turning the other cheek, well, no one slapped Eggplant Charlie or would dare to think about slapping Eggplant Charlie, so that point seemed to be moot.

"Bones, am I dying?" asked Eggplant Charlie from his hospital bed in the ICU.

"I'm afraid so, son," responded Bones, showing his compassionate side.

"Are you real Bones? Are there any real doctors here Bones?" asked Eggplant Charlie.

"You were dreaming, son."

"I was flying."

"Of course you were."

"I need something from you, Bones."

"Damn it! Do I look like a damned candy striper to you?" *Ah, that was better* thought Bones.

"Remember the days in the line, Bones? It's me, Mister Tambo. I got a favor to ask."

The ante-bellum appeal rang a bell inside the old demon's skull, and he again felt slightly compassionate toward Eggplant Charlie.

"What is it son? You want me to send in Walt Whitman?"

"No, no, no. Please don't."

"What is it then?"

"Tell them a squirrel bit me, not my wife. Tell them Bones; I'm begging you!"

"Well, I'm not much good at communicating with a bunch of goddamned baboons. I'm a doctor, damn it, not a politician."

"Bones, I'm begging you!"

"I'll see what I can do," said Bones, with an eye toward getting Eggplant Charlie to shut up.

At that point, the pretty doctor from central casting entered Eggplant Charlie's room and sat down in the chair next to his bed. She looked worried.

"You've got a high fever and the wounds aren't closing up the way they should be," said the lady doctor.

"Tell'er Bones!" said Eggplant Charlie.

"Tell me what?"

"It was a squirrel, lady. The man was bit by a squirrel, not his wife," said Bones, in vain.

She seemed to ignore Bones completely and asked Eggplant Charlie once again, "Tell me what?"

He was just able to get the words out. They were just barely comprehensible, but she could understand most of them.

"A squirrel bit me. I was bit by a squirrel."

"A squirrel?"

"Yes, a squirrel!"

She thought about it, and decided that it might be possible, but how? How could a person be in a position to be bitten this severely by a squirrel?

"How is that possible?" she asked.

"I held it up to my face!" said Eggplant Charlie.

"Well, that was stupid," said the doctor despite herself, whereupon Bones attempted to chide her for her bedside manner.

"Lady, people don't go to hospitals because they do smart things to themselves!" he scolded.

She wasn't listening. The doctor had always distrusted anger in both its righteous and ungodly forms. Whether she *couldn't* hear Bones or *wouldn't* hear Bones is debatable. The point is that Bones had nothing much to do with helping Eggplant Charlie get his point across. The urgency was all about Cauliflower. The semi-righteous old demon had proven himself irrelevant once again.

Now if this were a medical show on T.V., the narrative might run something like this. The doctor realizes that the patient was bitten by a squirrel and has fallen victim to ardillian paralysis, a life threatening state involving delusions and hallucinations, not to mention drastic fluctuations in blood pressure and brain wave activity. Fortunately, it is completely treatable with the right cocktail of prescription medicines, the patient would show signs of improvement within a couple of days, a duration that would be shrunk by television to a couple of minutes. Then, right before the patient's release, the doctor would wink at him and say something cute like, "Now don't be picking up any more strange squirrels." There would probably also be a positive change in the patient's attitude. Having gone through a life threatening episode, he would be a kinder, gentler soul from that point on.

The problem with all this is the problem with modern medicine. The analysis of cause and effect is superficial. The doctor had understood that Eggplant Charlie had been bitten by a squirrel and had, consequently, developed symptoms that seemed to fit within the parameters of ardillian paralysis syndrome.

Her mistake was that her analysis of both the cause and the effect was inadequate. She would have done better had she taken her analysis out of the passive voice and instead of having started with the premise that *Eggplant Charlie was bitten by a squirrel,* had started with the premise that *a squirrel bit Eggplant Charlie.* If she had thought about the cause in the active voice, she may have bothered to ask herself "*Why?*"

Now, she had asked *how* it was possible for the squirrel to bite Eggplant Charlie's face multiple times, and Eggplant Charlie had told her that he picked it up to look at it more closely.

Instead of asking w*hy,* she passed judgment on Eggplant Charlie, proclaiming his action "stupid." Bones had attempted to correct this behavior, but she couldn't see him, and she wasn't listening.

Bones was beside himself in anger, literally. Righteous Bones had temporarily split from ungodly Bones, and they were both fuming. After a couple of seconds, however, they were reunited into one entity again. Bones, in his anger, didn't even notice that he had just split like an amoeba.

"Goddamn doctors today are all a bunch of idiots," he said. His own track record as a physician while he was drawing breath was actually much worse than that of Eggplant Charlie's doctor. He never spent much time on analysis because there wasn't much to analyze. A patient had been shot, so the arm or hand or foot or whatever would have to come off. After Bones had ceased drawing breath and during his probationary period as a righteous ghost, and even later during his post-probationary period as an inept demon, he hung around hospitals a lot, and to his credit, he learned a lot about modern medicine from what he saw.

Of course, Bones was also informed by his post three-dimensional experiences. He could have written a critique of modern medicine a million pages long about what doctors didn't know about the human condition and the causes of their patients' torments and distress.

"Ask him why, lady!" he said in disgust. She wasn't listening. Eggplant Charlie had written Bones off as unreal, but he was equally frustrated with the doctor.

Immediately after Eggplant Charlie was finally able to communicate that a squirrel had bitten him, the doctor had an "aha" moment.

"Aha! Ardillian paralysis syndrome!" She then hurried out of the room in order to go about the business of fixing Eggplant Charlie.

The doctor could not see the metaphorical elephant in the room. The doctor was oblivious to Cauliflower. The problem was Cauliflower.

The doctor had seemed to understand that a squirrel had mauled eggplant Charlie, but she didn't seem to care much about what that entailed. The squirrel mauled Eggplant Charlie. Therefore, Cauliflower did *not* maul Eggplant Charlie. Eggplant Charlie desperately wanted the doctor to find out what had happened to Cauliflower, but the doctor, afflicted with modern medical tunnel vision, thought her patient's wife was of no particular interest, now that she could be excluded as the cause of her patient's condition. After all, she wasn't a social worker.

WHY? Sam the squirrel bit Eggplant Charlie because he was afraid. Sam was afraid because he had been injured moments before. To put that last sentence in the active voice, Sam was afraid because Eggplant Charlie had seriously injured him moments before. Eggplant Charlie threw a rock at Sam because he heard Sam chattering. Eggplant Charlie was infuriated at the chattering because…well, at this point, the cause and effect becomes less definite and more mysterious, but the real cause *of*, and the real solution *to* Eggplant Charlie's current state of distress could only be determined if this information were to be made available, but by whom?

The passive voice is good for dodging blame---"*Mistakes were made*", or for focusing on the effect— "*The patient was bitten by a squirrel*", but the passive voice is, by design, really inadequate for identifying a cause or an agent.

The doctor didn't care about the agent. Her patient had been bitten by a squirrel and had been diagnosed as having ardillian paralysis syndrome. She had the solution, so she arranged to have Eggplant Charlie's bloodstream infused with a cocktail to knock it out.

It knocked Eggplant Charlie out right away. In fact, you could say that it killed him, in that his heart stopped beating and he stopped drawing breath.

Sam wasn't exactly angry. He felt the way he usually did when a female squirrel he was chasing ran faster than he did and thwarted his copulation plans, or when another squirrel found his stash of acorns. He felt as if he had failed.

What was new was that the failure was a communication failure. Squirrels usually don't much care if other squirrels understand them or not, but for some reason, Sam did, right then.

They didn't understand his dialect. Okay, no problem. They understood "special dirt," but they didn't understand that "special dirt" and "pine needles" were metaphors for heaven.

Sam made ten voiced glottal stops in rapid succession, which in any squirrel language means, *"No! Stop it!"*

The universal quality of this message does not necessarily indicate that all squirrel languages are descended from a single, primitive language which we might be inclined to call *Proto-Squirrel*. The universal use of ten voiced glottal stops in rapid succession among squirrels is similar to the human expression *"Okay"*, which is of obscure origins, but has managed to spread to the extent that people say "Okay" in Beijing and Buenos Aries and Tripoli. Well, the squirrels rolling in the pine needles in the woods behind the State Line Veterinary Associates' office knew from the newcomer's utterance that Sam thought that things were not okay.

They regarded Sam with suspicion. He was a foreigner, after all. They had long forgotten that it was Sam who had taught them to roll in pine needles. Now, he was just some jerk who seemed to be telling them that rolling in pine needles was bad. Maybe he was *not-squirrel*. Maybe someone should bite him a lot.

Although squirrels talk, non-verbal communication makes up the lion's share of their discourse. There is far more universality in regard to squirrel gestures than there is regarding squirrel words. When sixteen squirrels put all four feet on the ground and look directly at another squirrel and flick their tails spasmodically, it means the other squirrel is facing a lynch mob.

Stickle surveyed the scene with disgust. Squirrels weren't much better than humans. Maybe they *were* just rats, after all.

The anointed one, the squirrel who would bring the notion of heaven to all squirrels, was presently on the verge of martyrdom.

"Sam Squirrel is all squirrel!" clucked Sam in his own defense. "All squirrel is Sam Squirrel. Bite me, Bite all squirrel."

Unfortunately, conditional sentences don't translate very well, and squirrels have little use for them, even in their native dialects. Of course, Sam meant something like, *"If you bite me, you are, in effect biting all squirreldom,"* but Sam couldn't have produced a sentence like that for all the acorns in Maryland. What he really said, of course, was "Bite me, bite all squirrel," and unfortunately, the hostile squirrels glaring at him with their tails a-twitching could only understand the "bite me" part, which they took as an invitation. They ran at Sam, who fled for his life, past the boundaries of the woods behind the State Line Veterinary Associates and across County Road 323, which was fairly busy.

One driver who had come all the way from Wilmington to buy eggplants from the co-op was frustrated to find that they would be unavailable until further notice. His frustration manifested itself in his driving. He drove just a little too fast down County Road 323, unimpressed by, and uninterested in, the bucolic, but somewhat ordinary, Mid-Atlantic countryside.

The driver saw several squirrels dart out in front of him, and he heard his tires make contact twice, which made him cringe. He looked in his rearview mirror and saw two squirrel bodies lying on the hot asphalt, both with tails twitching, and he felt eaten up with guilt. He thought briefly of turning around and running over them again to put them out of their misery, but then, on second thought, he realized that would be disgusting. *Oh well. They're just squirrels. They're basically just rats, and the woods are full of them.* The driver was thankful that his daughter was not in the car with him. It would have upset her no end to see her father kill a couple of critters out of anger-inspired negligence. He glanced up at the sky and said, "I'm sorry. Forgive me"

Sam was suffused with a profound feeling of gratitude, which is an extremely rare emotion among squirrels. The gratitude was directed externally, but Sam had no words to describe to what or to whom the feeling was directed. All he knew was that Twenty-Seven-Slow-Clicks-At-Half-Second-Intervals and his girlfriend, whose name Sam had forgotten, had been chasing him and then they became not-squirrel.

The other squirrels in the lynch mob perceived that there was no percentage in pursuing Sam across County Road 323 after seeing what had happened, so they scampered on back to their side of the road. The memory of Twenty-Seven-Slow-Clicks- At- Half – Second- Intervals and Five-Sustained- Clicks –Followed- By-A- Voiced- Glottal – Stop (which was his girlfriend's name) did not even fade. It just disappeared. Squirrels do not mourn.

Lying there on the hot asphalt, Twenty-Seven-Slow-Clicks- At- Half – Second- Intervals reflected on his situation. "*Not squirrel me Twenty-Seven-Slow-Clicks- At-Half – Second- Intervals.*" His dying girlfriend called out to him, "Rolling in special dirt..." Then, their tails stopped twitching. As they left the three dimensional realm of mortals and immortals, leaving their not-squirrel carcasses for the crows and possums, they were not burned by asphalt nor filled with fear as the differentials of dozens of vehicles passed over them. They sensed the aroma of pine needles and briefly experienced something similar to what Eggplant Charlie had during the flying dream, only for Twenty-Seven-Slow-Clicks- At- Half – Second- Intervals and Five-Sustained- Clicks –Followed- By-A- Voiced- Glottal – Stop, it was no dream.

Stickle felt like a complete failure. He felt his flask for reassurance, but he did not take a pull from it. He was tired, or, more accurately, he was weary. His life had been sad, and his afterlife was turning out pretty miserably as well. He decided to go for a long walk down a dangerous road.

In life, he had been attracted to heights and he liked to stand on the edge of the deck when traveling by steamship. When traveling by train, he always walked a little too close to the track. These behaviors were not technically suicidal. He never jumped on to the path of an oncoming train, but he found it oddly comforting to flirt with those notions from time to time.

His fatal fall from the rooming house balcony was, by the way, purely accidental. He was far too drunk at that time to flirt with anything or anybody, let alone flirt with danger.

The dangerous path upon which Stickle had chosen to tread had a name. It was called Interstate 95. Cars and trucks sped down the road at eighty or even ninety miles per hours. While Stickle was drawing breath, the fifteen-mile-per-hour speed of a locomotive seemed unnaturally fast. In this brave new world, however, going four, five or six times faster than that unnatural speed was considered an ordinary thing.

Walking down I-95 is truly dangerous for the living. Such a stunt could even be seen as a manifestation of a suicidal tendency. For Stickle, however, the danger was even greater. In the movies, they often show "ghosts" as having no substance, and, therefore, objects and people can pass right through them with no harm done. This is inaccurate. If Stickle stood in the middle of the highway, he would have caused a trans-dimensional collision. His status would be downgraded, and he would have had to re-enter the cycle of rebirth at a very low level, possibly as a worm or an amoeba.

If a vehicle were to hit him, the vehicle and the driver and passengers would also suffer damage, though the causes and effects of these kinds of damage would not be apparent to those drawing breath in the realm of mortals and immortals. The car might stall mysteriously six weeks later, for example, or the driver might suffer a pinched nerve many years after the collision. For this reason, responsible "ghosts" do not put themselves in positions that could cause these trans-dimensional catastrophes, so walking down I-95 was quite a reckless thing for Stickle to be doing.

"Mind if I join you?"

Stickle instantly recognized the voice of his old friend. They had met while Bones was a surgeon in the military field hospital in Washington and Stickle was a volunteer. Actually, Stickle only volunteered for a couple of days, but

Bones did not hold that against him. Bones had no patience for those who cried or ran away at the first sight of blood, but Stickle didn't do either of those two things. Stickle, despite the brevity of his stint, was actually quite helpful as he mopped up blood, disposed of disembodied limbs or administered whiskey to a patient undergoing surgery. Stickle wasn't a coward or a quitter, but he wasn't made for the job, unlike Walt Whitman, who clearly was.

Although Bones was grateful for Whitman's help, he never liked the man precisely because he was so good at that horrible job. In Bones' opinion, far too many people were good at their horrible jobs. The president was good at his horrible job. The generals were good at their horrible jobs. The soldiers were good at their horrible jobs. Bones was good at sawing bones, which was a horrible job. The nurses were good at their horrible jobs.

Stickle was not cut out for his horrible job, and was much better suited for his wonderful job, which was writing pretty songs. Bones saw it and respected it. After work, the two would play cards and drink and sing, Bones knowing all the time that the acquaintance would not last long.

One day, as Bones was sawing through a young man's thigh, the soldier died of shock. Stickle was assisting the operation. After making sure that the body was respectfully removed and that the operating area was relatively clean, Stickle looked around, shrugged, and walked out of the building, never to return. Another surgeon hollered after him.

"Come back here, you lily-livered old drunken coward. Your country needs you! Come back and do your duty!"

"Aw, leave him *be*!" shouted Bones with such natural authority that the other surgeon not only shut up, but felt a deep sense of embarrassment for having popped off in the first place.

Now, many moons later, the two misfit spirits were walking down I-95 together. The Bones that manifested himself to Stickle wasn't a black man in a Starfleet uniform, nor was he dressed as a Civil War surgeon. Although he was completely recognizable to Stickle as Bones, the form he chose this time was that of a twenty-first century motorist carrying an empty gas can.

"You're not very frightening looking for a demon," observed Stickle.

"I'm not much of a demon, I guess. I took this form because I figured it'd make it less likely for you to get your silly ass recycled into that rebirth mess," explained Bones.

"How's that?"

"They see a fellow with a gas can, and they won't pass someone on the shoulder and hit someone else who's not really there," clarified Bones.

"Good thinking. So, they can see you, huh?"

"Yeah. I got nothing to lose. I'm officially a God-damned demon now. They can all see me. They don't seem too concerned, though."

"Well, I guess this isn't a very good place to chat. Let's go get a drink," suggested Stickle.

"Fair enough. The trucks will still be here tomorrow, just in case we feel like jumping in front of one. I got a gallon of Saurian brandy in this gas can. I think you'll be amused by its presumption."

Jubal Early Djumich and Thaddeus Stevens Chen had a few things in common, but they hated each other, nevertheless. Jubal and Tad were both born to history buffs in Cecil County, Maryland, and they were named after players in the great conflict that divided the sympathies of the residents of the so-called "Free State", which was, in reality a slave state.

They both attended Cecil County Community College and earned Associate's Degrees in criminal justice. They were both employed by the Cecil County Sherriff's department. They were both sent to investigate reports of a possible stabbing behind the State Line Veterinary Associates building, and they both ended up being shown in the viral video seen 'round the world.

They weren't video stars, mind you, but they played more than bit parts in the drama. Tad Chen provided something of a voice over—"*Suspect appears to be hysterical,*" etc., while Jubal Djumich tased the crazy lady.

It wasn't that Officer Chen disagreed with Officer Djumich's decision to tase the stabbing suspect. It just seemed a little too predictable that Jubal would resort to using the taser. Officer Chen noticed that Officer Djumich seemed inordinately fond of his new high tech weapon shortly after it was issued to him.

Although they didn't like each other very much, the two cops often found themselves at similar social events, if you could call them social events. These events mostly involved drinking beer with other cops, since non-cops neither trusted cops enough, nor were trusted enough by cops, to join these gatherings.

Cops at these gatherings tended to separate into two groups. Cops like Tad Chen liked to drink beer, talk dirty and go home. Cops like Jubal Djumich liked to drink beer, race each other down country roads, and shoot up stop signs.

Tad Chen thought Jubal Djumich was an ignorant redneck who was not really any better than the people he tended to lock up on Saturday nights.

Jubal Djumich thought Tad Chen was a goody-two-shoed nerd who was not really any better than the Sunday school teachers who used to ruin his precious weekends when he was an elementary school student.

One evening, by a pond just off County Road 284, after draining a number of cans containing Coors, Officer Djumich said, "Hey watch this!" an expression which made Officer Chen wince since it was so often a prelude to something dangerous and stupid. Then, Officer Djumich tased a goose.

"What the hell!" yelled Officer Chen, who could not abide any cruelty to animals. He ran at Officer Djumich.

"Bring it on, you store-bought bitch!" hollered Officer Djumich.

The two started fighting in the goofy, many-holds-barred style of middle-school males. The other cops pulled them off each other and made them shake hands, but the animosity remained. It didn't help that the goose had died.

Officer Chen was no rat. The tacit cop code of conduct prevented him from tattling on Officer Djumich. The cops in this cohort gave each other carte blanche when it came to drunk driving, pot smoking and discharging firearms at inanimate public property. The murder of a human being or a bank robbery, of course, would not have been given a pass.

Tasing a goose to death was somewhere in the middle. Had it been a dog, Djumich would have been beaten bloody by all the cops at the roadside gathering, and he probably would have found his work environment to be too hostile a place for him to continue to be employed. Had it been a cat, he probably would have escaped unscathed, at least physically, from the wrath of his peers, but he would have earned a reputation as a sicko.

Instead, it was a goose, but not a farm animal. It was a Canada goose, a member of a species that seemed to be making a transition from wild to quasi-domestic. With the advent of global warming, these geese had started to hang out all year in the Mid-Atlantic, instead of going back and forth from Canada to Florida like the wealthy Quebecois humans known as *snowbirds*. Whereas the public perception of Canada geese was formerly one of respect, it was beginning to turn to one of disgust. Their gross, greenish, excrement was ubiquitous around local ponds, and their increasing dependence on humans and the man-made environment was beginning to change their status from picturesque game to pestilence.

For this reason, there were two separate hunting seasons for Canada geese—one for the migrating variety, the noble savages flying south in Vee formations each fall, and one for the ne'er-do-wells, fouling ponds and scaring kids with hissing and wing-flapping and other territorial behaviors.

Most of the cops were hunters, and hunters have a code, too. You are not supposed to shoot an animal just to see it suffer. Well, Jubal Djumich had clearly just done just that. However, since the animal in question was kind of a fat rat with wings in the minds of a majority of those who were gathered that evening, the consensus was that it was lapse in taste and judgment rather than an act of sadism.

Both officers would be given a pass. Officer Djumich would be pardoned for his irrational exuberance since he had just been issued a particularly cool new toy, and Officer Chen would be pardoned for throwing a few punches at

Officer Djumich because, what the hell, guys punch each other sometimes.

Several months after the tasing of the goose, Officer Djumich drew his taser and discharged it in the line of duty and in the presence of Officer Chen. Officer Chen didn't see it as excessive force, *per se,* but it wasn't the exactly the way he would have handled the situation. He let it go, partly because he did not want to open up old wounds. As his Tong gangster ancestors would have said, *"Bury the hatchet!"* Officer Chen reflected, "Aw well, I guess it's better that the idiot shot her with a taser than with a real gun."

"**Lilith**, what's wrong?" asked Mark Metacomet. Lilith was sitting at the counter of the Seattle-style coffee shop on Main Street known as *Witches' Brew.* Mark Metacomet had been looking for her, and he had finally discovered her here, nursing a latte all red-eyed and snuffling.

"Great. Now I got a stalker," she said.

"There are worse things than being stalked. Shoot, I'd love to have a stalker. Instead, I'm just plain old Mark Metacomet, a natural-born rock star doomed to eternal obscurity."

"Aw, poor baby. Your feeling sorry for yourself doesn't help me out a bit!" replied Lilith to Mark Metacomet's unsuccessful attempt at consolation.

"Sorry about that. I'm sorry about everything. I saw something really strange when I was in the bathroom at the Old Post Road Inn."

"I saw something too, when you were running out of the bathroom," said Lilith with a smirk.

"Yeah, I got busted for it too. I forgot to tuck it back in. I saw a …well, forget it. It wasn't really there."

"You know, I hate men. I hate you sons of bitches."

"That's okay, Lilith. I hate men, too. A lot."

"I lost my job because stupid Dan loves Cauliflower."

"I love Cauliflower, too. A lot."

"Why are you here?" asked Lilith.

"Because when I was sitting in my jail cell after getting busted for indecent exposure, the ghost of a nineteenth century songwriter told me that my soul was not in harmony with the universe, and that I had better get together with you to get Cauliflower out of her jam, or it would be bad, in terms of karma, for both of us," explained Mark Metacomet.

"I can't stand Cauliflower," stated Lilith, either ignoring or accepting Mark Metacomet's bizarre explanation. All hippies talked that way sometimes. They weren't to be taken too seriously.

"Why not?"

"Cause she's such a stupid screw-up."

"Oh, and you're not? I say that respectfully, cause I definitely am."

"Oh that's news, all right. Running around naked and landing in jail, and now you're telling me you're a screw up. Do tell."

"That's right, and so are you."

"Okay, I'll bite. In what way am I a screw up?"

"You lost your job at the co-op. It's the only job you could ever keep because you're such a bitch, and no one else would have you, and it wasn't even a real job, and it didn't even pay real money. Honey child, we're both screw ups and neither one of us is getting any younger or any cuter, and neither one of us is made for this place and time," responded Mark Metacomet.

"Everyone is trying to straighten me out these days. Bertha the Lesbian Roofer told me that I didn't have the qualifications to join the lesbian club."

"I've got no idea about that. I'm not trying to get you to join anything. I'm not trying to get you, period. I'm not after what I was after the other night."

"And what was that?" asked Lilith.

"Your sweet loving charms."

"You don't want them anymore?"

"Nope. No offense."

"Why not?"

"I'm on a mission. I got something to do."

"What?"

"Rescue Cauliflower."

"I hate her."

"All the more reason to rescue her."

"How do you figure?"

"Love your enemy and save yourself."

"Where didja get that?"

"From the Word. From everything that's been coming my way lately. I've always known that money wasn't where it's at. I decided to play music instead of plying my trade, which is plumbing, or using my education; I got a B.A. in psychology. Why? I knew that money wasn't where it's at. I had to be true to my own self, and so I've tried, but I found myself writing mean little stupid songs about the honest hard-working people I knew, and I knew that wasn't right either. I'm not a great musician. I'm not a great plumber. I'm not any kind of psychologist. I'm just a bozo asking you on bended knee to help me save someone who has never done anyone harm."

That part about Cauliflower having never done anyone harm didn't sit right with Lilith, somehow. There was bad chemistry between her and Cauliflower, and she didn't know where it came from.

That's the way it is with bad chemistry. Where does it come from? Why do we like some people and hate others? It has nothing to do with righteousness. We like "bad" people and hate "good" people sometimes.

It may have something to do with unaddressed grievances in the cycle of rebirth, but how ignorant is that? Should we really be hating people for the stuff they did a thousand years ago?

The fact was that Lilith had no good reason to hate Cauliflower, and she knew it.

Lilith was attached to some silly little demons, but even she could see how small and ridiculous they were. She looked at them as they really were, right then, and decided that they were not worth listening to. Mark Metacomet, however, was making a little bit of sense.

"Listen, Lilith. The viral video was a bunch of crap. Eggplant Charlie got bit by a squirrel, and Cauliflower is an innocent victim of the World Wide Web."

"Huh. So, how do you plan to go about fixing it?"

"By telling the truth. It'll work," replied Mark.

It always does. The truth stings and stinks and burns and purifies. The truth cauterizes and cleanses. The truth is the truth, and its power transcends dimensions. Mark Metacomet knew that once he and Lilith were committed to spreading the truth, nothing could stop them. They would get shed of their demons and would be in a position to help Cauliflower, and, in the process, to reclaim their own souls. The problem was that Lilith wasn't quite convinced yet.

Saurian brandy comes from the imagination of the people who created a 1960's sci-fi series. Nevertheless, it is palatable to "ghosts" and demons, who can "smell" and "taste" it, albeit not in the way that mortals can smell and taste. Stickle and his old pal Bones, who was now thoroughly drunk and re-transmogrified into a Civil War doctor, sat at a picnic table at a rest stop on I-95, just over the Delaware state line, sipping the stuff.

Stickle was cautious. His conversation with "Demon" Alcohol had not been for naught. He sniffed the brandy to make sure that the substance was the essence of fellowship rather than the essence of attachment before he imbibed.

"So here we are, stuck between heaven and hell. Lord, have mercy. What are we going to do?"

"Do you mean for ourselves? Does it matter?"

"Of course, I mean for ourselves, and of course, it matters."

"I'm on a mission. I'm trying to save a bunch of squirrels," said Stickle.

"Do you how that mission started?" asked Bones. "Let me tell you, because I know. They were just getting ready to downgrade my status, and they were adjudicating your case. You had gotten completely drunk, and you had fallen asleep right there in Celestial Court."

"I don't remember any of that."

The Saurian brandy might as well have been lemonade. Stickle was as sober as a judge as he listened to the tale of his judgment.

"Yes. They liked you. Your songs charmed heaven itself. They didn't want to pitch you back into the cycle of rebirth, but there you were in court, joined at the hip to demon alcohol, just as you had been when you were drawing breath, and you were snoring away."

"That's awful."

"That was funny. I laughed. It got me into a little trouble, but I didn't care. You are so bad at everything except for what you're good at, Stickle. You make me laugh."

Bones was drunk. Stickle was sober and trying to get the straight story about a time when Stickle was drunk and Bones was sober. If it really was the straight story, it might explain a lot, but Stickle had to be careful. Bones was a demon, after all, and demons are supposed to cause trouble, and they don't mind stretching the truth.

Bones seemed to anticipate Stickle's apprehension.

"Don't worry, Stickle. *In vino veritas.* I'm telling you true, and the truth can't do any real harm. I know I'm a demon, but I'm really bad at this horrible job. I'll talk more about that later."

"Yes, please," responded Stickle. "Tell me more about what happened in Celestial Court."

"A heavenly choir sang your songs. The judges smiled; the angels danced. The Buddha cried when he heard *Hannah Slumbers 'Neath the Sweet Gum Tree.* Then they talked about what a lousy husband and father you were. You weren't there to defend yourself. You were too drunk. I asked for permission to advocate for you, and they said it was okay. I reminded everyone that the Buddha had left his wife and baby to seek and spread enlightenment, so the hangtag of 'deadbeat dad' should not be applied to people like you who spread enlightenment with their artistic endeavors. They were impressed with the argument, but they couldn't get around the fact that you were too drunk to speak on your own behalf."

"Then what happened?" asked Stickle.

"Then you came to. You should have stayed out, cause you were one grouchy, smelly, hungover jerk!"

"What did I do?"

"It wasn't what you did. It's what you said. You said that you couldn't understand why heaven had let humans suffer in darkness. You asked why it was so hard to enlighten people when all they had to do was describe heaven to them. Then you said, and I quote, `In the time it has taken you to enlighten human beings, I could have enlightened every damned squirrel on the planet.'"

"Oh no. I must have been really drunk."

"What else was new?" asked Bones, rhetorically.

"What happened?"

"They deliberated, and you know the rest. They gave you your status, which wasn't all that bad. Your songs saved you from the cycle of rebirth, but you had to pay for the contempt that you showed your Celestial judges. That was the part I couldn't live with," said Bones, shaking his head.

"What was the penalty? I've forgotten."

"They told you that you couldn't enter heaven until every squirrel on the planet had a shot at understanding the concept of heaven. You had to teach them so that the wheels would be put in motion for the squirrels to enlighten one another, and so that peace and harmony would reign throughout all squirreldom in the three dimensional realm of mortals and immortals.

Well, as your attorney, I couldn't stomach that. `This is a travesty!' I shouted. `Why not ask him to teach cows how to tap dance, instead?'

Well, my case was next. I was on probation already, and I was fixing to lose my status as a righteous ghost for shouting out loud at an incompetent doctor during an operation. Everyone could hear me. I knew that was wrong. I just lost my temper. Now, there I was, losing my temper at the same beings who would pass judgment on me! Stickle, I'm a dope!"

"Maybe," said Stickle, "but I think you're a righteous dope."

"Well, I'm supposed to be a demon. That's what they said. They appreciated what I had done in the war, and that creep Whitman spoke glowingly of me, but that didn't change the fact that I had brought anger with me wherever I went, nor did it change the fact that I had cursed heaven in anger.

A righteous ghost should ascend to heaven after his mission is completed. Thing was, I'd screwed up my mission and blown my second chance at the Celestial hearing. I wasn't allowed to re-enter the cycle of rebirth, not even as a virus. I was supposed to go and serve the powers of darkness, but I can't stand those sons of bitches. Didn't like 'em in life, like 'em even less in death. Sad thing is though, on account of that sentence, I really am a demon. Even when I try to do right, it comes out wrong. I always act out of anger, and even though I got plenty of righteous anger, I got a store of ungodly wrath as well, and that ungodly wrath informs far too many of my actions."

"I had a sense of my mission, but I don't remember it being put forth so explicitly," said Stickle.

"Yes, they mostly communicate these things through telepathy. It's more efficient that way. They don't waste as much paper, so to speak."

"Squirrels, huh?"

"That's it. You know, I have a confession to make. I've been screwing you up recently," said Bones.

"You have? I must say that that seems rather out of character for a being who is enduring damnation for sticking up for me in Celestial Court."

"Like I said, I try to do right, but the demonic nature kicks in and it all goes haywire."

The other side of the county road was yet another wild and wonderful place. Sam had entered a suburban development. The trees were exotic samples of trees one might find in Asia, Africa, Europe, South America, and even Australia. Sam had never seen their like. The squirrels were different, too. They seemed more adventurous and much more willing to explore their *not-squirrel* surroundings.

Dogs and cats lurked, and there were plenty of cars around. Sam espied one *not-squirrel-that-was-once-squirrel* -- a phrase that he had coined during his preaching days – and surmised that although this brave new world was a garden of earthly delights, it was fraught with danger, and it certainly was not all *rolling in special dirt*.

Sam saw a male squirrel chasing a female up a telephone pole and across the telephone line. Sam's mouth was agape in admiration. The squirrels here were different, and maybe better. Maybe they would understand.

Lilith looked up from her latte and said, "All right. Let's see. You want me to save Cauliflower and restore her reputation. Since I can't stand her, and since I'm not really crazy about you, would it be okay to ask what's in it for me?"

Mark Metacomet smugly replied, "It'll help you save your soul."

"Not interested," replied Lilith.

"I'll do anything you ask, Lilith. I mean it."

That changed everything. When you offer to do anything a person like Lilith asks, you are really offering quite a lot.

"That changes everything. I accept, under one condition."

"I said *anything.*"

"You are to be my love slave for a week, after which time I'll probably be bored with you, so then I'll set you free to pursue anyone who'll have you. I've got to warn you, though, I guarantee you'll be damaged goods after a week with me, and I'm not so sure it'll be so easy for you to find that special someone."

"Your wish is my command, Lilith."

"Don't call me Lilith. You are to address me as Your Celestial Highness."

"As you wish, Your Celestial Highness."

Lilith slapped him hard across the face, making a few customers choke on their cappuccinos.

"You are not to speak unless you are spoken to, worm!"

And so on. Thing was, Mark Metacomet kind of liked this stuff. It was brand new, and it seemed to scratch an itch he hadn't even known he had. Hot dog!

At this point in a hospital not so far away, Eggplant Charlie was dead, but that does not mean what it used to mean. In Bones' Civil War days, dead was dead, and he carried this unambiguous view of death with him into the fictionalized future of the 1960s sci-fi series. "He's dead, Jim," he would say with great finality.

Fortunately, the pretty doctor from central casting did not subscribe to the he's-dead-so-let's-call-it-a-day attitude expressed by the quasi-demonic starship medical officer. She would go to great lengths to prevent Eggplant Charlie from entering the afterlife, especially since her anti-ardillian paralysis syndrome cocktail seemed to be responsible for his current condition, which we could call *flat-lining*. She brought in the various devices used to jump start a flat-lining patient. Meanwhile, Eggplant Charlie was having an out-of-body experience.

It was a whole lot like the flying dream. He looked down at the scene below with the doctor and the jump-start equipment and decided he would fly or swim or float over to see Cauliflower, wherever she was.

He didn't get very far. Stickle grabbed his ankle out in the hallway and pulled him back to Earth.

"Gotcha! Where do you think you're going?"

"I want to see Cauliflower."

"If you float too far away from your body, I'll guarantee it'll be the last time you see her. I thought you said she needed you."

"She does," said Eggplant Charlie, who was suddenly uncomfortably aware that the need was mutual. He was suddenly very cognizant of *his* need for her.

"Yeah, well, it's not easy helping people when you're a ghost, and that's if you even get to be a ghost. You'll probably have to re-enter the cycle of rebirth, anyway. Most people do. You'd be lucky if you could hold it together well enough or long enough to say goodbye forever to her."

"So what should I do?"

"Go back and try to help the doctor bring her back any way you can," said Stickle.

Eggplant Charlie was usually rather stubborn about things he knew about. However, he knew when the voice of experience was talking, and when it was wise to shut up, listen and do what he was told. He floated back over to the room in which his body lay. He was touched to see tears in the doctor's pretty eyes. Something was odd, though. Everything was frozen.

Stickle said, "Yes, we are in a time interval. We can do this because we are dead. Our time doesn't have to be *their* time. I thought I'd slow things down a little so we could chat."

"So there's no harm in what's happening now?" asked Eggplant Charlie.

"None," said the righteous "ghost".

"Let me ask you a question. It's obvious to me that everything I've seen over the last couple of days hasn't been real. You've always seemed real, so let me ask you this, Mister Stickle. Are you real, or are you just a symptom?"

"You know, it's quite ironic that you of all people are asking me this. Who or what the hell are you?" asked Stickle.

"I'm an organic farmer from Cecil County, Maryland," responded Eggplant Charlie.

"An earth-hippie, a back-to-the-land guy, huh?"

"You've been dead quite a while. If you're real, how do you know about earth hippies and the back-to-the-land movement?"

"I read the papers," replied Stickle honestly. Libraries are full of "ghosts". "So," he continued, "are you farming to save the earth?"

"I guess, in part, I am," replied Eggplant Charlie.

"Well, your farm is an ecological disaster; did you know that?"

"How do you figure? It's certified organic."

"It's an ecological dead zone. You've declared war on biodiversity. You only want the species to thrive that you can sell at the co-op. You may not use herbicides and pesticides, but in your cucumber patch, you only tolerate cucumbers, and heaven help any other kind of plant or animal that should chance to sprout there or wander through it."

"So I'm a rotten plant killer, and all farmers are enemies of the planet, huh?"

"You know the suburban development where you grew up?"

"Sure."

"If you could have seen that development sixty years ago, you would have seen a treeless landscape. The only plants growing there were stalks of corn. Then, the farmer sold his land. The so-called "cookie-cutter" houses that were erected afterwards were criticized and sneered at. You know what the development looks like now?"

"Yeah, kind of."

"It's a forest! An oxygen producing, carbon-dioxide consuming forest! There are deer, foxes, and raccoons everywhere. For the first time since the Pilgrim fathers arrived, the land is covered in forest, and people are living in harmony with it," explained Stickle.

"So, I'm destroying the planet, and the soccer moms and the office drones are saving it?" asked Eggplant Charlie, dubiously.

"That's one way to look at it, but that's wrong too. Your problem isn't your job. People need you. They need high quality food, and you produce the best. You are a gifted man, but like a lot of gifted people, you have an attitude problem."

"How's that?"

"Running an organic farm does not make you a better human being than those you call soccer moms and office drones. You're part of the same civilization they are. You haven't really dropped out of anything, and you know it. You advertise on the internet, for goodness sake!"

"You know about the internet?"

Stickle looked annoyed. "Yes, and horseless buggies and iron birds and magic moving picture shows, too. My body may be buried, but I've been walking through this vale of tears for a hundred and eighty some odd years, give or take."

"Sorry, I guess it's the suit."

"I could change it, but I think it fits my personality," said Stickle.

"Do they have dry-cleaners in the afterlife? Would it hurt the effect if you smelled a little better?" asked Eggplant Charlie.

"I hadn't noticed, but then, again, I'm dead." Does the smell bother you now?"

"No."

"That's because you're dead, too. I'm not attacking you, Eggplant Charlie. I'm just taking a couple of nanoseconds to point out the error of your ways, and I think you'd better listen."

"I'm all ears."

"Your problem is your attitude. You're no better than anyone else."

"I know."

"You're worse in some ways."

"Okay."

"Well, quit acting like you're somehow superior. You're just as parasitic as everyone else is toward Mother Earth. Thing is, Mother Earth doesn't mind."

"How do you know?"

"Have you ever heard of the Hadean Era?"

"No."

"From 4.5 billion years ago to 3.8 billion years ago, seven hundred million years, give or take, the surface of the earth was four hundred and forty six degrees Fahrenheit. How's that for global warming? If every human being on the planet drove an air-conditioned Sherman tank, and all the ice in the world melted, it still wouldn't hold a candle to what Mother Earth has already been through, and what it will go through years from now."

"How did you hear of the Hadean Era?"

"I've had a lot of free time, and I'm interested in geology. What I'm trying to tell you is this—all the attempts to preserve and save the earth are pointless in and of themselves because the earth will survive the experience of being home to humans just as it survived the experience of being home to trilobites. These attempts only make sense when you add people into the equation. Save the planet for the people—for future generations. Save it so the quality of life will be better, and so that people won't suffer so much."

"All right, I'm sold. Can we look for Cauliflower now?"

"Not right yet. Remember, we got to get you drawing breath again first. Now, tell me again why you want to find Cauliflower."

"She needs me."

Eggplant Charlie could detect the phoniness in his own tone of voice. He knew he wasn't telling the whole story, and he knew that there wasn't much point in trying to deceive a being like Stickle.

"And?" demanded Stickle.

"I need her," replied Eggplant Charlie.

"Why?"

"I have no idea!"

"Well I do," said Stickle. Let me tell you about a conversation I had with a half-hearted demon who used to cut people's arms and legs off for a living."

"As I said, Mister Stickle, I'm all ears."

"**O**h, Celestial Majesty! This miserable cockroach, who does not deserve to lick the divine foulness off the pointy end of your boot, which you use so exquisitely to kick this undeserving wretch where he needs to be kicked, requests permission to speak."

"Then speak, worm!"

"If we're gonna make this happen, I'll need my gig back."

"You really think they are going to rehire you the Old Post Road Inn after you danced your little jig last time?"

"Yeah, and I need to go back there and get my stuff anyway."

Now, it's better that the circumstances of this conversation are not described in detail. For example, it's best not to describe what they were wearing and not wearing. Suffice it to say that Mark Metacomet looked a little similar to the Mark Metacomet fleeing the giant mouse. Lilith was dressed, and undressed, completely differently than she had been that fateful evening.

There was a palpable change in both of them since that evening, however. They were both having some fun for a change, and, consequently, their moods were improving in spite of their perverted selves.

Cauliflower was recharging. Visitors such as the doctors who were making their rounds and the medical students, who padded after them like puppies, were no longer frightened or disturbed by her appearance. She seemed to be sleeping, as two of her eyes were closed. Her third eye, however, was wide open, and she was in a state of awareness that most of us will never be able to experience. She radiated calmness as she waited for her body to regain the energy she would need to put this situation to rights.

Sam couldn't help himself. He started preaching again. He was starting to fancy himself as a squirrel of words, and here he was, chattering away to the squirrel community in this suburban development. As they performed their acrobatics, Sam was awed again and again. These were the bravest, most graceful, and happiest squirrels he had ever encountered.

As it turns out, their dialect and Sam's were mutually intelligible if not identical, so much so that they understood Sam's preaching, or seemed to, although they didn't gather in pine-needle-rolling circles at his feet to hear him.

Instead, they kept at what they were doing, but when they ran close to Sam they would click, "Good" or "Right" or "You're in the right tree now!" Sam was well pleased.

Poor old Bones was confessing.

"So this mission of yours… well, I tried to help, and I, being the demon that I am, I made a mess of it."

"That's okay," said Stickle, graciously. "I think I'm eternally in your debt anyway for advocating for me in Celestial Court and even for your being outraged at the results of the hearing."

"No, I really messed you up. You know that guy we've been messing with?"

"Eggplant Charlie?"

"Is that his name? The guy who thinks he's Mister Tambo in my minstrel line?"

"Yes, that's him."

"He's a returning celestial being."

Stickle knocked his glass of Saurian brandy over in shock.

"That man?" said Stickle. "He volunteered to return to earth out of great compassion? He hates everybody!"

"Yes, he's a different breed of cat, all right. He's a hard one to figure out, but yes, he was in heaven, and he volunteered to get his memory cleaned out and be sent back because he saw the distress the human race was in, and he thought he could help out."

"By growing vegetables and throwing rocks at squirrels?"

"Well, the last was my idea."

"What do you mean?"

"I sent him that thought telepathically. You'd been trying to talk to that damned squirrel, and he wasn't understanding beans, so I though a little rock therapy might help."

"You used a returning celestial being to throw a rock at a creature? That would violate his Buddha-nature and put him at the level of those doomed to re-enter the cycle of rebirth. Nobody deserves that! But a celestial being?!"

"I know; I know. I was trying to help you out, but I forgot that I was a demon, and that I couldn't do good even if I wanted to."

Stickle thought about correcting Bones' grammar. "*Couldn't do <u>well</u>, you mean,*" he almost said, but he realized

"...*do good*" was what Bones had meant. *Good* was a noun here, and the object of the verb *do*, so it shouldn't be changed to *well*. Sobriety was having a weird effect on Stickle. Grammar suddenly seemed very important to him.

"So now we have a dying Buddha who will probably be reborn as a worm in one of his own apples. That's screwed up Bones, I'm sorry. I still can't get around the idea that this man was a Buddha once. What's the story there?"

"He was drawing breath in the three dimensional world of mortals and immortals fifty thousand years before the present day. He was living in Europe, one of those Cro-Magnon people. He was born into a hunter-gatherer lifestyle, and he provided well for his family, but he gathered rather than hunted, and was so good at it that he always had plenty of fruits, nuts, berries and edible plants to trade for animal protein. He was a rare bird in those days because he managed to avoid killing."

"So he became a Buddha just because he didn't go hunting?" asked Stickle.

"No, that wasn't it. At that time there were two different kinds of humanoids occupying Europe."

"The Neanderthals and the Cro-Magnons," volunteered Stickle, always eager to prove that he was a man, or former man, of science.

"Am I telling this story, or are you?" snapped Bones, demonically.

"Please, continue."

"The Neanderthals and the Cro-Magnons. You could say that the Cro-Magnons survived and became us, and that the Neanderthals went extinct, but that's not quite what happened. The Neanderthals were overwhelmed, and most of them left no genetic legacy, but apparently there was some intercourse, both social and sexual betweem them and the Cro-Magnons because white folks and Asians still have a little of their D.N.A. By D.N.A. I mean…"

"Bones, I know what D.N.A. is."

"Really!" Bones was genuinely impressed. "Anyway, about fifty thousand years ago, there was a lot of what you could call racial strife between those two groups. The Neanderthals were definitely at a disadvantage. Their technology wasn't as advanced. Their language wasn't as expressive. They relied a lot on telepathy and intuition for communication, neither of works as well as plain old talking.

The Cro-Magnons didn't much care for the Neanderthals, and they didn't much like sharing their resources with another human species, so it was always kind of open season on Neanderthals.

Things really got bad for them right about the time old Tambo got his wings. It seemed that a bunch of Cro-Magnon chiefs had gotten together and decided to wipe out the rest of the Neanderthals. They spread the word that Neanderthals were pretty good eating, too, so there were a lot of pretty gruesome barbecues back then.

Well, somehow our mutual friend was able to face down the various chiefs at a big Cro-Magnon powwow. He must have had a lot of charisma or something. He told everyone there that Neanderthals were humans and that eating them was cannibalism, and that they needed to share resources with them and learn about what they had to teach because they had been around long before the Cro-Magnons.

He finished his oration with a command, `*Let them _be_!*' and for several thousand more years, that's exactly what the Cro-Magnons did in regard to the Neanderthals. They let them *be*. Well, sooner or later, Neanderthal society began to crumble, and individual Neanderthals began to join Cro-Magnon bands. Eventually, there were no pure-blooded Neanderthals left, but they live on in modern day humans because all non-Africans have a little of their D.N.A.

The guy who made such a perfect appeal to the better angels of Cro-Magnon nature impressed heaven enough to release him from the cycle of rebirth and allow him to enter paradise.

His old lady, who had preceded him in death by a few months, was waiting for him there. She had been with him all along, supporting him and giving him the courage of his convictions just by *being* there."

About fifty thousand years later, when he volunteered to return to earth out of compassion for humanity, he understood the conditions. There would be no memories of his previous life or of heaven. He would have to start from scratch again. The idea was that anyone who prevented a genocidal holocaust would probably be of great service during the late twentieth and early twenty first centuries."

"It turns out he is just an organic farmer. Strange huh?" commented Stickle.

"It happens that way sometimes," explained Bones. "The celestial beings regress to the mean and do not achieve anything close to what they had achieved in their past lives. The powers that be usually let these cases back into paradise without a lot of fanfare. They get credit for what they did time before last."

"But if they screw up….?"

"They can get sent back into the cycle of rebirth. They can even get claimed by the powers of darkness and become extra-powerful demons. I knew I had done something awful when I got a note from my demonic superiors congratulating me on a job well done. I'm truly sorry, Mr. Stickle," said Bones.

"What can we do now?" asked Stickle.

"We? Well, I'd best stay out of it. But if I were you, I'd get down to the hospital. That silly bespectacled beauty queen has got some twenty-first century miracle fix for ardillian paralysis syndrome that's going to kill him dead. Tell him to resist it! His disease is spiritual in nature, damn it! Not biochemical! He's got to get back in the game!"

The manager of the Old Post Road Inn beheld the freak show before him. Lilith was dressed in black leather, fish-net stockings and spiky high heels. She was not, however, carrying a whip, for which the manager was grateful.

Mark Metacomet was wearing a sleeveless tee-shirt with an arrow on it pointing in Lilith's direction and with the caption, *I'm with the Diva of Discipline.* He was wearing what appeared to be surgeon's scrubs for pants. *Easy on, easy off,* thought the manager. Mark Metacomet was also wearing flip-flops for shoes, the purpose of which, evidently, was to show off the fact that his toenails had been polished with a different day-glo color for each little piggie. His fingernails were similarly styled. He had had his left nostril pierced, as well as his left earlobe, and now there was a chain of hoops leading from one to another. He had false eyelashes in one eye *ala* Kubrick's *Clockwork Orange,* and his hair, which was long before, had now been fashioned into a Mohawk, which was somewhat appropriate given his Native-American origins. He never had a mustache before, but now a Salvador Dali style curlicue was grease painted onto his upper lip.

The most disturbing part of these outfits, by far, was what connected them. There was a doggie leash attached to the spiked weaning collar around Mark Metacomet's neck. Lilith, of course, held the other end.

The manager recognized them both instantly, and decided that he didn't really know either of them well enough to inquire about their private lives, even though it seemed as if they were doing their level best to make their private lives public. He thought he'd talk to Mark Metacomet because even though he was the more bizarrely attired of the two, Lilith was clearly the more frightening.

"Guess you're here to get your guitar, huh? It's in the back. I'll get it for you. I guess I still owe you something for your last night here, too." The manager wanted any unfinished business with Mark Metacomet to be concluded as quickly as possible.

Lilith elbowed Mark Metacomet in the ribs loud enough for it to be audible. He let out an involuntary groan of pain, and briefly flashed a smile, which was an involuntary manifestation of pleasure.

"Speak worm! Did you bring your owner here for nothing?" Lilith asked rhetorically.

The manager briefly wondered if he should call the S.P.C.A.

"Thanks, but maybe I could play here again this weekend. I'm feeling a lot better now, and I've made some changes to the set that I think the folks will like," said Mark Metacomet.

The manager couldn't help himself. He started laughing, and he couldn't stop. Lilith tugged at Mark Metacomet's leash as if he had tarried at a fire hydrant too long and now it was time to get back to their stroll down Main Street.

Finally, the manager spoke. "Okay, I'm dying of curiosity, but you know the weekend crowd is earth hippies, not leather freaks. Keep your clothes on, okay kiddies?"

Mark Metacomet replied, "I'm real sorry about last time. It was an accident. It wasn't part of the act. Thanks for this. I won't let you down. You won't be disappointed."

"That's enough!" snapped Lilith. "He said you could come back. Why are you still talking? Have you turned into a little chatterbox now?"

Much to the mangers amazement, Mark Metacomet was completely silent after that. The manager had never pegged him as the submissive type before, but maybe he wasn't such a good judge of character.

"Well Mark, I'm glad you got the girl you were hitting on, but you know the old saying—*Be careful what you wish for*. Looks to me like the fly is chowing down on the spider, and the spider likes it that way. Aw well, to each his bone, I guess. Now I mean it when I say keep it clean this weekend. A little *Rocky Horror* is fine, but I don't want to see any Marquis de Sade. By the way, I'm on kind of a losing streak, so I'm gonna try that trick of your running around with my pants down to impress the next woman who strikes my fancy. Sure seems to work for you!"

The manager was not usually such a smart-ass, but he felt obliged to stick up for Mark Metacomet in his degraded current condition. It pained the manager to see a fellow male human being so thoroughly humiliated by the likes of Lilith.

Lilith, again to the manager's amazement, did not throw anything at him or stalk out after his comments. Instead, she smiled, and actually laughed a bit.

"You know," said Lilith, "you really might want to try it, and I think it really does work for him."

The manager realized something about this pair. Despite themselves, they emitted an aura of pure happiness, and it was contagious. Whereas they were both creeps before, ironically, now that their creepiness had come out of the closet, they were palpably less creepy.

The manager laughed too, and said, "See you kids later." He realized he was actually looking forward to it. Lilith smiled again and said, "Bye-bye," and Mark Metacomet offered up a "Woof!" Wow, common courtesy—saying hello and goodbye and acknowledging a fellow human's existence. How out of character it was for both of them, and what a pleasant change!

The sign for Friday would have to be changed. It had always been a joke before, advertising "*Mark Metacomet and King Phillip's Revenge.*" The joke was that Mark Metacomet had no band. He was a solo act. The Wampanoag chief's revenge was supposed to have taken the form of the mean little lyrics that "Indian" Mark Metacomet had made up about the descendants of those who had dispossessed his seventeenth-century ancestor. The ironic thing was that the earth hippies were mostly descended from Irish, Italian, Anglo and Slav immigrants who had come to the New World long after King Phillip had gone to his reward. Some of their ancestors had crossed the Atlantic below decks, in chains. Some of the earth hippies were, by blood quantum at least, every bit as Native American as Mark Metacomet.

Now, Mark Metacomet wanted to change the sign to reflect his change in attitude. He erased the old sign, which was written on a chalkboard placed on an easel. He changed it so it read: "*This Weekend: Mark Metacomet and Community Service!*"

Floats- Like- A- Butterfly was not a Native-American although some of her descendants would be, thousands of years after she died. The fact that the English translation of her name would be used as part of a famous boxer's motto, also thousands of years later, is completely irrelevant.

Floats- Like- A- Butterfly was a native of the Iberian Peninsula, but, as she was part of a semi-nomadic group, she spent most of her life in what people would later call France. She didn't speak French. She spoke a dialect of a language that was spoken by almost the entire Cro-Magnon population of Southwestern Europe at that time, and she could also make herself understood in the regional Neanderthal tongue, and was fluent in many animal languages including the local dialect of Squirrel.

Floats- Like- A- Butterfly was well thought of among the members of her band and among the members of other bands who would convene on solstices for what we would describe as powwows today. In a way, she was the Cro-Magnon counterpart of what Jackie Kennedy was to many Americans during the nineteen sixties. She had grace and culture. She was soft spoken and kind, and had a powerful charm that disarmed all who met her.

Her mate had no official title and was not exactly the chief of any band, but many Cro-Magnons held him in higher esteem than they did their own chiefs, not for his oratory prowess, but because of his brilliant and revolutionary lifestyle. He was a renaissance man who lived more than forty nine thousand years before the Renaissance. His credibility was based on what he did, not what he said.

Together, they were a primitive power couple, but their power came from within and from each other, not from public acclaim.

Floats- Like- A- Butterfly was an artist, and some of her sketches of animals can still be seen today on the walls of caves. Most of her work, though, was done on hides and woven pieces of fabric, and have long since rotted away. What has survived could hardly be called her best work, but her talent is clearly evident in the surviving pieces as well.

Her mate, Has- A- Knack- For- Flint- Knapping, was a craftsman rather than an artist. All of his creations were utilitarian in nature. Years later, archaeologists would examine some of his handiwork and recognize that a revolution in technology had taken place, since stones, unlike hides and fabric, do not rot.

Pre-historians divide the so-called "Stone Age" into the Paleolithic, Mesolithic, and Neolithic periods, meaning, unimaginatively enough, old stone age, middle stone age, and new stone age, respectively. If they could see all that was made during these periods, it is doubtful that they would use the term "stone age" to describe any of these eras. In fact, they might call the period during which Floats-Like-A- Butterfly and Has-A –Knack- For- Flint –Knapping were alive and kicking the Vegetable Matter Age, since plant matter accounted for a good bit of the stuff used to create shelter and clothing. In addition, the fruits, nuts, berries, tubers, shoots and leaves gathered, usually by the women, made up the bulk of the Cro-Magnon diet.

Now, Has-A- Knack-For-Flint- Knapping was a renaissance man, but "renaissance man" is a term relative to the savagery of a certain time period, and that time period was relatively barbarous. It was common then, for example, to decorate the entrance to one's shelter with one's former enemies' heads on sticks. Has- A Knack- For- Flint- Knapping considered that bit of décor aesthetically unappealing. Instead, he found flowers with thorny stems, flowers ancestral to present-day roses, and transplanted them in from of his hut in lieu of the customary display of crania so popular at the time. It seemed crazy, but it worked.

Floats- Like- A- Butterfly liked certain kinds of edible plants, and used other plants for weaving fabric. Has- A- Knack- For- Flint- Knapping transplanted those as well.

No, he wasn't the father or even the great-great-great-grandfather of agriculture. That so-called revolution began many thousands of years later. He was a pioneer in horticulture, however, inasmuch as he had a garden. That garden enabled him to stay home and experiment with new ways of chipping stone, which is also called knapping flint. He didn't have to hunt. He grew most of the food he needed, and he traded the spear points, awls, scrapers, fish hooks and other stone tools that he made for meat.

Floats- Like- A- Butterfly actually befriended a small band of Neanderthals who hung around, semi-parasitically, her band of Cro-Magnons. They would utilize Cro-Magnon cast-offs because the second-hand, discarded Cro-Magnon tools, clothing and shelter materials were still of higher quality than those created by Neanderthals.

The Neanderthals were pretty good at hunting and fishing, however. Enough so that most Cro-Magnons thought of them as a threat to their way of life. Nevertheless, Floats-Like- A Butterfly sought them out, not for trade or personal gain, but simply because she was curious about them.

One day, a hunter appeared at the entrance of her shelter and announced that he had meat to trade for some stone tools and fabric. Floats- Like- A- Butterfly told the hunter that Has- A- Knack- For Flint- Knapping was out just then, but that she could see what they had to trade. The man reached into his satchel, a large one crafted by Floats- Like-A- Butterfly herself, and pulled out a couple of arms and the head of one of her Neanderthal friends.

Floats- Like- A- Butterfly was not usually given to fits of rage, but this time, she picked up a large branch and drove the hunter off. Then, she doubled over and vomited and cried bitter tears.

Has-A- Knack- For- Flint- Knapping did not quite feel the same sense of outrage as did Floats- Like- A – Butterfly, but he agreed to take up her cause when it was his turn to speak at the next Cro-Magnon powwow.

Cro-Magnons were not like squirrels in that they gave some credit to the innovators of new ideas and technology.

Has- A- Knack- For- Flint- Knapping had earned credibility for his innovative tool making techniques, his supply of vegetables and fabric, and, last but not least, his glamorous and charming wife. No one would dare deny him his turn to speak at the powwow, though what he said would not be accepted by everyone.

"Thank you for hearing me. I am Has-A- Knack- For- Flint- Knapping of the Ibex Clan, who belongs to the tribe of Those-Who-Can Attend- The –Solstice- Powwow-without- Getting- Killed. I need to speak to you about something that some of us have been doing that's not compatible with what it is to be one of Those-Who-Can Attend- The –Solstice- Powwow-Without- Getting- Killed."

Heckling is a very old human tradition. It is only about twenty minutes younger than public speaking, itself, and since Has-A- Knack- For- Flint- Knapping was not universally loved, a heckler soon called out.

"I'm keeping my heads. Try taking them away from me."

"Brother," replied Has-A- Knack- For- Flint- Knapping, "although I prefer to decorate the front of my own dwelling with thorny flowers, I have never suggested, nor will I ever suggest that a man does not have the right to cut the heads off his enemies and put them on sticks. The way you choose to decorate your home is your choice and your choice alone. I think we can all agree, however, that *eating* one's enemies is wrong."

Some of the older listeners in the crowd were slightly embarrassed. It hadn't been so long ago that cannibalism among this group of Cro-Magnons had not been considered taboo that some couldn't remember the taste of fresh enemy liver.

"What are we arguing about, then? I don't eat my enemies. I'm not a damned savage."

"That's my point. We are not savages. We are Those-Who-Can Attend- The –Solstice- Powwow-Without- Getting- Killed. And yet, someone of our tribe tried to trade me the meat of some of the People-Who-Steal-Our-Garbage for some tools and fabric."

There was a hush in the crowd. No more heckling. Has-A-Knack-For- Flint- Knapping had touched a nerve. Quite a few people had at least tasted some of the new meat, and more than a few thought it was pretty good, and that its consumption provided an elegant solution to the competition for resources problem that was one cause of the animosity between the two subspecies of humanity.

They hunt where we hunt, so there's not as much game as there was before. Why not hunt them? Why not eat them? They're not quite human, and they taste good.

"Why not eat them? They're not quite human, and they taste good," called another challenger.

"What makes them not quite human?" asked Has-A-Knack –for- Flint- Knapping.

"Their tools aren't as good," responded the challenger.

"My tools are better than my neighbor's. Does that give me the right to eat him?

"They're uglier."

"Do better looking people have the right to eat uglier people? Do more intelligent people have the right to eat slower people? If so, we all need to fear becoming someone's dinner. The only person who is safe is the most intelligent, best-looking person with the best set of tools. By deciding that the People-Who-Steal-Our-Garbage are less than human, we make ourselves less than human. I have said what I came to say. I am nobody's chief. I cannot force others to accept my way. All I ask is this—if you kill any of the People-Who-Steal- Our- Garbage, please don't use a spear point that I made, or one that you made following my design. I made them to make our lives better, not worse. Please do not use the choppers I designed to butcher the flesh, and please do not try to trade the meat of the People- Who- Steal Our Garbage for our vegetables or our cloth, for I fear that Floats- Like- A- Butterfly would ask me to cut your head off and put it on a stick, and I do not want to hear her say something so rude and out of character. Thank you again for letting me speak."

The speech was a success in that the crowd didn't turn into a lynch mob, and killing and eating Neanderthals did eventually go out of fashion although the practice didn't end completely while Has-A-Knack- For- Flint- Knapping was drawing breath.

Has-A- Knack- For Flint- Knapping and Floats- Like- A- Butterfly ascended into heaven where they were welcomed by other celestial beings. However, the rules were not as strict back then, and Has- A- Knack- For –Flint- Knapping took an attachment with him, which was needing to see a job finished. This type of attachment is typical among craftsmen. Others are more able to start a project and then leave it to others to finish. This, of course, is the best way; otherwise, projects that require more time than a lifetime affords would never reach completion.

Has- A –Knack- For Flint- Knapping wanted to return to earth to perfect humanity, but his motivation wasn't philanthropic or selfless. He really wasn't motivated by great compassion. He felt he had started something at the Cro-Magnon powwow fifty thousand years ago, and he wanted to see it through.

Floats-Like- A- Butterfly understood this perfectly well. Her soul mate was a good man and a clever man, but he had no great love for other people besides her. He simply liked to do things for the sake of getting things done, and to make things for the sake of making them. He didn't like hurting people or animals, and he wanted to create rather than destroy, but he had had nothing but disgust for many of his Cro-Magnon countrymen and what he perceived as their savage habits. He didn't love them as they were, but maybe he could fix them. Maybe he could take these rough rocks and fashion them into beautiful spear points.

Floats- Like- A- Butterfly was successful in dissuading him for about fifty thousand years, but she finally relented and said he could go, under the condition that she would go too.

"But there's no guarantee that we'll be born in the same place or that we'll meet up with each other," said Has-A- Knack- For- Flint- Knapping.

"Yes, there is. You have my guarantee. It would be a violation of the laws of the universe if we were not together."

She was right. He was reincarnated into the misanthropic farmer known as Eggplant Charlie, and she became known as Cauliflower, or the blood soaked woman on YouTube who shouts about squirrels.

Eggplant Charlie was having a revelation, the kind that often happens to those caught in this kind of limbo. It was kind of a *déjà-vu* revelation. It was the feeling that he had been there before but it was was hazier than most of that ilk. He had been *here*, meaning this planet, but not in this particular hospital. He had flashes of who he once was and what he once did.

"I was kind of a farmer before there were farms, and I was good at working with flint," he said to Stickle.

"That's what I heard son. Bones, from the minstrel line, mentioned that," Stickle replied.

"Cauliflower doesn't deserve this crap. She's only here cause of me."

"That seems right, too. I'm sorry to say," said Stickle.

"Am I missing anything?" asked Eggplant Charlie.

"Yes, indeed. Your soul is in danger. You've got to get back in the game. That doctor wants to help you, but she can't do it alone. She needs your help. She'll feel awful if she kills you with that stuff she pumped into you. Your disease is spiritual, and you can't fix a body without a spirit. Get the hell back in there, boy, or I'll sic Walt Whitman on you!"

Eggplant Charlie didn't understand the Walt Whitman reference, possibly because there never was a cartoon version of *Specimen Days* featuring Mister Magoo, but he understood that there would be hell to pay if he didn't come back to life, so he jumped back into his body, even though the doctor was giving it electric shocks at the time, and it was a painful and unnatural feeling. Greater love hath no man than this: that a man forsake a beautiful floating sensation to deliberately jump into a body that is being electrically shocked.

He was no longer flat-lining. The doctor was an emotional wreck. She cried and hugged Eggplant Charlie, and said, "I'm sorry. I thought I knew what was wrong with you. I'm so sorry!"

Eggplant Charlie was feeling pretty charitable for a guy who had just been dead and who had just been jump-started.

"No problem, Doc. No harm, no foul."

"Don't worry. I'll find out what's wrong with you, and I'll get you better."

"I'm fine. You stitched me up. I'm not bleeding anymore. That's all you have to do. I don't even have a fever anymore." And he didn't.

Eggplant Charlie continued, "So listen. If you really want to help me, just get me out of here. I have work to do. I have to go and find my wife."

His wife! The doctor had forgotten all about the poor man's wife and how she had been falsely accused of mauling him.

"Listen, your heart stopped a few minutes ago. I can't let you go anywhere. I need to keep you here for observation."

As brave and determined as Eggplant Charlie was, and as strong as the bonds that tied him to Cauliflower were, he found that he didn't have the strength to resist or protest any further. Being dead, remembering past lives and talking to ghosts can really take the wind out of one's sails.

Officers Chen and Djumich, to their mutual chagrin, had been made patrol partners again. Their dislike for each other was not hatred, so they both were attempting to make the best of it. The video hadn't exactly changed their lives, but everyone at the Sherriff's Department had seen it and knew that Officer Djumich was the cop in the video who tased the vampire woman. The two were now driving down the quiet streets of Elkton, literally looking for trouble, and more out of boredom than affability, Officer Djumich decided to make small talk.

"You think it was wrong?"

"What are you talking about?" asked Officer Chen.

"The video."

"Yeah, they shoulda never posted it."

"Nah, I mean what *we* did."

"You mean when *you* tased her?'

"Yeah."

"What do you think?"

"I don't know. I think maybe it was wrong, but she looked nuts."

"Yeah, she was whacked out all right."

"So you're okay with what happened?"

"Yeah. You did what you did. It's over. The dude's in the hospital and the lady's in the nuthouse. All's well that ends well. Forget about it. Let's get some coffee."

Bones didn't want to do what he felt he had to do, but he figured he owed it to himself. If he were truly a demon, looking purity straight in the eye would blind him and maybe even send him out of existence in most of the realms he inhabited. *I'll probably still appear in the re-runs of the sci-fi series*, he thought to himself. "Well, here goes nothing," he said aloud as he pushed open the door to the room in which Cauliflower was lying in restraints.

Sam was ecstatic with a kind of joy that no squirrel had ever felt before. Squirrels never seemed to have much of importance to say, and they all figured that all squirrels basically thought about the same kinds of things, so, as a rule, they didn't worry much about being misunderstood. Sam, however, had done some traveling in his short life, and he felt he had an important message to impart, so he felt frustrated when he was misunderstood, as he had been in the woods behind State Line Veterinary Associates. Now, he was experiencing the opposite emotion. He was in ecstasy because he seemed to be understood by the squirrels in these new surroundings.

The Celestial Court had made Stickle's job almost impossible in several ways, the most obvious being that squirrels were not particularly open to new concepts. Another significant problem was that Stickle had to teach the concept of heaven without ever having seen it for himself.

Stickle knew it existed, just as he knew, say, California existed. He'd heard about it, read about it, and listened to descriptions, but he no more really understood it than one can really understand what it feels like to ski down a mountain or scuba dive in crystal clear water without having personally experienced these things. Experiencing heaven vicariously wouldn't seem to be much of a credential for teaching about it, yet Stickle was relatively good at it, "qualified" or not.

A few of his songs, the ones that didn't dwell on sadness and dipsomania, combined imagery, rhyme and melody to produce a hint of heaven that was understandable to mid-nineteenth century Americans, who didn't really need anyone to teach them about hell, for the hints about that place were legion.

Like the medieval paintings that showed hell in great detail and heaven as sort of a waiting room, the preachers at tent revivals could ramble on for hours about the misery that awaited the unrepentant. Bad as things were sometimes in this realm, the tortures that awaited the damned were much worse.

In their defense, most of these preachers were motivated, at least in part, by a genuine concern for other people's souls. The preachers were what shamanistic societies describe as "medicine men", and they administered strong, scary medicine to all who came to revivals. The thing is, strong, scary medicine often *works* on people who are, spiritually speaking, very sick. Many lost souls can testify that their lives were turned around after hearing a certain imam or priest or preacher or rabbi. Perverts, thieves, murderers, and drug addicts have all been, at times, transformed by tales of fire and brimstone, or were they?

The fire and brimstone provided the catalyst for the change in these folks, but a part of them had to be open to what they were hearing. Something opened their ears and hearts, and what really worked on them was usually not the threat of eternal torture, but the promise of escape from their *present* hell, the one which they saw every day.

If the sermons were only about torture, then the preachers were really demons, for demons communicate through causing pain. When one person wrongs another, the party of the second part hears the voice of a demon saying, "*Show that jerk how it feels!*" When adults attempt to teach children not to bully by smacking them and rhetorically asking, "*How did that feel?*" they are imparting a demonic lesson. When poor old Bones thought he was helping out Stickle by having Eggplant Charlie peg a rock at Sam, he was simply thinking along demonic lines, and, paradoxically, trying to do good.

Powerful medicine is for very sick people. An imprisoned murderer, for example, is not likely to turn his life around after a few visits from a Unitarian chaplain. However, most people are not that sick, and fire and brimstone is not what they need to escape the endless cycle of rebirth. You wouldn't give chemotherapy to a patient with a head cold. Likewise, scaring the wits out of basically healthy people every Sunday actually impedes their spiritual progress instead of accelerating or enhancing it.

A hint of heaven, though, seems to be a rare and special thing that has the potential to make life worth living. While he was drawing breath, Stickle saw, felt, smelled, heard and tasted hints of heaven everywhere, even when he was loaded. He infused his body of work with these hints, and those who listened to his songs picked up on some of them, and when they sang his songs, they were spreading the word every bit as effectively as Billy Sunday could in his wildest dreams.

The critic from the *New York Times*, who loved the video of Cauliflower on You Tube, thought that the purpose of art was to shock and disturb. He wouldn't have defined art as something created to be pure and pretty. Stickle, on the other hand, thought that the purpose of art was to uplift suffering people, but not to anesthetize them because suffering had its place and purpose, too.

Does it matter whose definition of art is the right one? Isn't the binary concept of *art* and *not-art* a whole lot like *squirrel* and *not-squirrel*? We need the full range, bad art, mediocre art and good art to help us determine what is good and what is bad. There may be a hint of heaven in a work of art that is not perceivable to a particular observer, as they say, *beauty is in the eye of the beholder.*

Nevertheless, it is safe to say that neither the urinal at the Paris Art Show of 1917 nor the viral video of Cauliflower had the slightest hint of heaven about them. They were devoid of heaven and were just stupid demonic celebrations of hellishness. As far as the art critic for the *New York Times* goes, well, as Bones noted after reading the article on the video, "Some people have a taste for shit."

Cauliflower, though in restraints, was a piece of work and a work of art. Her two three-dimensional eyes were closed, but her third eye was wide open, and she could clearly detect Bones as he entered the room.

Your average demon would have thrown his hands over his eyes and let out a blood-curdling scream if he had seen what Bones saw then, but Bones was not your average demon. The light was bright, but not blinding. He felt like a person who had worked in a dimly lit office all winter who had suddenly been transported to a beautiful tropical beach. There were spots before his eyes, and the "sun" was too strong, but it was good.

Cauliflower spoke first. "Hello. Why have you come?"

"I came to apologize," said Bones.

"What did you do?" asked Cauliflower.

"I was messing with Eggplant Charlie and it got out of hand."

"Where is he?"

"He's in the hospital. I'm sorry."

"Is he going to be all right?"

"I don't know. I'm sorry."

"Did I hurt him somehow?" asked Cauliflower.

"No, lady. He was bit by a squirrel."

Then, Cauliflower asked the question that Eggplant Charlie's doctor should have asked in the first place.

"Why was he bit by a squirrel?"

"He picked it up and brought it to his face."

"Why?"

"To apologize to it."

"What for?"

"For throwing a rock at it."

"Why did Eggplant Charlie throw a rock at the squirrel?"

"I put that notion in his head."

"Why would you want Eggplant Charlie to throw a rock at a squirrel?"

"To help my old friend out."

"What was your friend trying to do?"

"He was trying to teach squirrels the concept of heaven."

"How would getting hit by a rock help a squirrel understand heaven?"

"I don't know, lady. It was a last ditch effort. You know some Zen masters hit their disciples when they are trying to teach them the same thing. I thought it might work; you know, knock a little sense into him."

"Poor squirrel!"

"I'm sorry about the squirrel, too, lady."

"Well, Eggplant Charlie doesn't like squirrels much, so I'm sure it wasn't all your fault."

"Thanks, lady."

"Everyone calls me Cauliflower."

"Thanks, Miss Cauliflower."

"Sounds like you've been having a hard time. You don't have to feel so bad about making a few mistakes. I make mistakes all the time. I'm probably the worst worker at the co-op, and I'm always screwing things up in Eggplant Charlie's vegetable patches. Last week, I pulled up a bunch of carrots because I thought they were weeds."

"Yes, ma'am."

"So you don't have to feel so bad."

"No, ma'am."

"Well, thanks for coming to see me anyway. You're dead, aren't you?"

"I guess you could say that."

"And I've seen you on T.V., right?"

"I think so. I was a doctor on a spaceship."

"You were a doctor a long time ago, too, right?"

"Yes, ma'am. How did you know…?"

"Everyone makes mistakes. Those guys who started the war and who were shooting each other and all that didn't know the trouble they were causing," explained Cauliflower.

"No, ma'am," agreed Bones.

"They weren't trying to hurt you."

"What a mess they made! I can't even describe it!"

"You tried to clean it up," noted Cauliflower.

"As best I could."

Bones was silent for a moment. He felt as if he had just been through a hurricane and now the sky was bright blue with nary a cloud. Bones thought, "*They freed the slaves. All that pain was necessary. All that suffering was necessary. You can't get something for nothing. It had to be.*"

"Miss Cauliflower, should I just forgive them and let it go?"

Cauliflower just smiled. The answer was obvious.

"Is it too late for me, Miss Cauliflower? They say I am a demon and can do no good even if I want to. Am I doomed for all eternity?"

"I just volunteer at the co-op. I don't know that much about your situation, but you seem like a nice man who's been through a lot. I hope you go to heaven if that is where you want to go. I think the squirrel's okay. He looked a little funny when he was running away, but I think he'll be okay."

"If I don't go to heaven, I'm stuck here. I just want to be able to do good again. I just don't want to keep screwing people up," said Bones.

Cauliflower's third eye blinked. The other two eyes remained closed. Then, she spoke.

"You don't have to *do* anything. Just *be*," she advised.

Bones looked and felt troubled by her advice. Cauliflower saw that she needed to clarify something.

"Or *don't be*, if that's too hard," she added.

Bones felt incredibly relieved.

"Thank you, lady, Miss Cauliflower. I can't tell you how much better that makes me feel. I've got to be going now. I hope everything works out for you."

"Thanks, Mister. Get some rest," advised Cauliflower.

"I will. I promise," said Bones. And he kept his promise.

Officers Chen and Djumich had more or less decided to give each other passes. They didn't exactly like each other, but they were willing to explore any socially acceptable areas they had in common. It never quite worked. For instance, although both were football fans, Chen like the Eagles and Djumich liked the Ravens. That didn't mean that either of them were going to give up looking for common ground, After all, they were doomed to sharing a patrol car for the indefinite future.

They finally found something or someone they could bond over in the person of Redneck Davey, whose Reagan-era Toyota pick-up had just given up the ghost, and who was walking down County Road 517 looking rough.

He looked rough right then, and he smelled rough, too. You wouldn't think he had spent the entire day being called "baby" and "sweetie" by a bunch of females, but he had. After all, he had just put in nine hours working with a very strange crew of roofers, the majority of whom were female ex-cons.

Now, Redneck Davy could clean up perfectly well. He volunteered at the co-op on weekends, not because he needed the food and the discounts. In fact, Bertha the Lesbian Roofer would have been happy to have him work seven days a week for her. He just felt that he needed more genteel company from time to time, and when he was at the co-op, he was always neat and clean-shaven. That was Redneck Davey's version of Dr. Jekyll. From Monday to Friday, however, Redneck Davey deliberately looked as rough as possible in order to escape what he saw as sexual harassment from his co-workers. Therefore, he didn't shower, shave or change clothes for five days running each week. To Redneck Davey's disappointment, his attempt at being Mr. Hyde did not slow down the comments from the women on the crew. *"Baby you smell nasty, but I like it like that! Why doncha come home with me, and I'll give your sweet skinny ass a bath..."* And so on.

So, Redneck Davey looked homeless as he ambled down County Road 517 and as Officers Chen and Djumich drove down the same.

Now, Redneck Davey fit a profile. He looked like a drifter, the kind of guy bored cops scare up a bit to make sure they understand that they are marginal human beings. Officer Djumich, from the passenger seat, lowered the window and opened the conversation.

"Hey buddy. How ya doing?"

"I'm fine officer, thanks. And you?" answered Redneck Davey.

Now, that Appalachian accent was yet another signal that the cops could mess with this guy with no repercussions. *White Trash. Hillbilly. Redneck--member of a despised minority-- one that it's still okay to bully.*

"Mind telling me what you're doing around here?"

"No sir. My truck broke down about half a mile down the road. I'm walking over to my cousin's house. That's where I'm staying."

"Staying at your cousin's house. Huh. You got any crack on you, big boy? Got any meth?"

"Any what?"

"Are you back talking me? Cause we can make this easy or we can make this hard."

Well, Redneck Davey had taken about all the crap he could take that particular day. He sized up Officers Chen and Djumich and decided that they weren't all that scary compared to the women with whom he had just finished working.

"I think you got the wrong fellow. I'm not someone who's gonna bend over for a couple of peckerwood cops."

Officer Djumich's dander was up, and Officer Chen, like last time, was playing along. "*What the hell*," thought Chen. "*The guy's asking for it.*"

Both cops got out of the car and approached Redneck Davey. Officer Djumich reached for his taser.

"Hell, I know you, you bastard!" said Redneck Davey. "You're the son of a bitch who tased Cauliflower!"

That was enough to make Officers Djumich and Chen pause. They suspected there was more to this bum that met the eye.

"What are you talking about?" asked Officer Chen.

"Yeah, I recognize your voice too. You're the same damn two cops that tased Eggplant Charlie's old lady. I saw you both on YouTube!'

Aw, hell. This was supposed to be fun, a little exercise in power that the two cops could bond over and discuss over some beers. Unfortunately, this guy had seen them on YouTube, which meant he had a computer, which meant he wasn't homeless, which meant that harassing him could have negative consequences. What's more, the two were apparently getting some questionable publicity as it seemed that not everyone who saw the video thought the tasing was justified.

"Just come here and put your hands on the hood of the car," said Djumich.

"No. Go to hell. I'm going to my cousin's," replied Redneck Davey.

Officer Chen realized that he would have to talk to Officer Djumich, who was just dumb enough to tase this guy.

"Okay, hang on, pal," said Officer Chen. Then he turned to Officer Djumich and said, "Hey, Jubal, let me talk to you for a minute."

Then Officer Chen took Officer Djumich aside.

"Hey Jubal, this guy's got a computer. He's somebody."

"No way, man. I'm gonna teach him a lesson."

"Listen to me. He knew the lady by name. I think he's in with that co-op crowd. They got some connections, and they got some clout. I bet this guy's got a job."

"Yo buddy," called Chen to Redneck Davey, "You working?"

"Yeah, I'm working. I don't drive around all day in an air-conditioned patrol car."

"Who you working for?"

"Bertha the Lesbian Roofer," said Redneck Davey, proudly.

Both cops let out an involuntary "Damn!" at the mention of that name. If Bertha found out that one of her workers has been harassed and tased on a country road while minding his own business, she would have had cop for breakfast along with her biscuits, and the cops knew it.

"Sorry sir, I guess this was a mix-up. Like you said, we were looking for someone else. Can we give you a ride to your cousin's?"

"No, it's a nice day," said Redneck Davey despite the ninety degree heat. "I reckon I'll walk."

As Redneck Davey walked the six miles to his cousin's house outside of Rising Sun, he started signing a little song about himself. Tomorrow, he would go see Mark Metacomet's new act, and maybe, if he gave Mark Metacomet some lyrics about himself, Mark Metacomet wouldn't be as vicious when his number came up.

Redneck Davey, with his red-eye gravy,

Well his truck broke down

Pretty far from town.

Redneck Davy, I don't mean maybe

From the old co-op

Then he met a cop

Or maybe two damn cops

Fresh from traffic stops

Well, the cops were bad

They thought they was cool

Cause they took a cop course

At the fool night school

They said "Hey boy

You best not run."

They wanna shoot Redneck Davey with their damn stun gun.

Redneck Davey ain't rich,

But he sure ain't poor

And he sure wasn't gonna

Take their crap no more.

He said, "You shot Cauliflower,

And you caused her pain,

What the hell's going on

In your pea-sized brain?"

Well them cops didn't know

Just what they should say,

And they wished Redneck Davey

A very nice day.

"Come on, Redneck Davey

Won't you come inside?

And we'll give your highness

A very fine ride."

"No thanks," he said, "I need fresh air,

And the smell of turkey's too strong in there."

The six miles went like a stroll in the park as Redneck Davey marched to the song of his own creation. Granted, Redneck Davey was no Stephen Ray Stickle, but he had written a righteous ballad. He had also stood up for himself, and this incident made him realize that he wasn't so vulnerable after all. He liked who he was, and no Mark Metacomet, no roofing tough gal, and no ignorant cop could change that. All he had to do was get the damn Toyota running again.

The scene on Friday night at the Old Post Road Inn was a weird one, all right. Mark Metacomet, whose act had always been folk music and old pop songs, seemed to be branching out into punk rock and performance art, by the looks of things.

Most of the earth hippies who showed up were curious about what he would do for an encore after his last exit. He had no real fans in the room, unless you could count Lilith, who really couldn't have cared less about his music. The people who had shown up were there out of morbid curiosity.

The act didn't change much during the first two sets. It was still folk music. Everyone was waiting for the third set, which was the one during which he usually sang songs about the local characters.

When it was time for the third set to begin, he introduced himself.

"Ladies and Gentlemen, my name is Mark Metacomet, and I am the great-great-great-great-great-great grandson of Metacomet, or King Phillip of the Wampanoags, who did his level best to kill every honky in New England.

I'm not proud of that, though. Lately, I haven't been proud of anything. I deserve to suffer, and I deserve to be punished, and fortunately I've found someone who is willing to do just that."

There were some audible groans in the audience. *Too much information! Well, here it comes. Let's hope he keeps his scrubs on.*

"Let's just say, 'It hurts so good!' I'm a lucky man, and I know it. Anyway, let me tell you why I deserve this punishment."

Some people were starting to leave.

"It has to do with Cauliflower. I had a hand in ruining her reputation, and now, begging your indulgence, I'd like to try to restore it."

Everyone was paying attention now. Mark Metacomet started to sing *The Ballad of Cauliflower.* It was no Stephen Ray Stickle song. It did not charm heaven, but it did the trick. Metacomet did not cite the source of his information. No mention of a giant mouse or a "ghost" was made. The point of the song was that Cauliflower didn't hurt Eggplant Charlie, and that the video did not present an accurate account of what happened that day.

The people in the audience were left cold. It was all a little too strange. Nobody applauded at the end of the song, so Mark Metacomet did what millions of other bar musicians do when they get no audience feedback. He launched straight into another song, one that he thought would be a toe-tapper, an audience-grabber. Stickle had helped him pen the tune days before, while he was still in jail.

> *You're moving around in a circle,*
>
> *But you think you're walking down a straight line.*
>
> *You're thinking in three dimensions,*
>
> *But you're forgetting all about time.*
>
> *Well, here you go `round again*
>
> *For something that you did way back when.*
>
> *No, I haven't gone `round the bend*
>
> *When I say you're going `round again.*

The song was rousing, and the audience began to clap along as Mark Metacomet launched into the second verse.

> *You can take my word if you want to,*
>
> *Or you can take the word of the Lord.*
>
> *He said he who uses a sword to kill*
>
> *Is also gonna die by the sword*
>
> *Now, if you're thinking in three dimensions,*

You might not really think that that's true.

But you're fixing to go `round the bend again,

And I ain't gonna accompany you.

The crowd was completely with him as he sang the chorus again.

Here you go `round again,

For something that you did way back when,

No, I haven't gone around the bend,

When I say you're going `round again.

He began the final verse of the song.

Now, look into your sworn enemy's eyes,

And think about a previous life.

The person you have sworn to kill

Might have been your mother or wife.

Until we start to get it together,

And until we start to love each other

It'll be world without end, amen, amen,

And we'll be doomed to do `er over.

Before Mark Metacomet launched into the chorus for the last time, he called out, "Sing with me!" And they did.

> *Here you go `round again,*
>
> *For something that you did way back when.*
>
> *No, I haven't gone around the bend*
>
> *When I say you're going `round again.*

The crowd was animated now. It was involved, and it was completely with Mark Metacomet.

Now it was time to close the deal.

> "When I say `Free", you say `Cauliflower.' Ready? On three. One, two,..
>
> `Free!'"

"Cauliflower!"

"Free!"

"Cauliflower!"

"Free!"

"Cauliflower!"

Well, if nothing else, Mark Metacomet had managed to prove that he could still provide the tavern goers at The Old Post Inn with a fairly decent evening of entertainment.

Sam's message had gathered momentum during his stay at the development. Squirrels all around were still going about their business, gathering nuts, copulating, chasing each other and jumping, but now they were chattering Sam's message at the same time.

"Rolling in special dirt!"

"Good!"

"Copulating."

"Good, squirrel, good!"

"Jumping."

"Good. Good."

"Cats and dogs."

"No problem, squirrel, no problem."

"Cars."

"No problem."

"Falling"

"No problem."

"Good. Good. Good. Rolling in special dirt!"

"Squirrel is rolling in special dirt."

"I squirrel, you squirrel."

"All squirrel is *squirrel.*"

"No Squirrel is *not squirrel*"

"All squirrel is rolling in special dirt!"

These messages spread like wildfire across Cecil and New Castle Counties. Sam had learned something else while he was evangelizing. In order to cross roads without getting smushed, he could scamper up a phone pole and run down the line until the line crossed the street. These were great, exciting times to be a squirrel.

Eggplant Charlie's doctor finally understood that her patient's wife needed relief, so she went to the hospital annex where Cauliflower was in restraints. She met with the doctor in charge of her care, and they went together to check on her status.

Cauliflower radiated calm, as it was her unique gift to be able to do so. Indeed, she had just been able to give peace to a restless spirit who had been walking the planet, eaten up with anger, for a hundred and fifty years. The dope they had given her had long since been neutralized by sleep, meditation, and sheer will. She even smiled as the two authority figures in white coats entered the room.

"How's Eggplant Charlie," she asked.

"Charles Tambeaux is doing much better now. How are you?"

"I'm really tired, and it's hard for me to sleep with all this stuff on me," said Cauliflower.

The doctors conferred and decided it was better to err on the side of caution, so although they released her from her restraints, they still held her for observation.

Newly freed, Cauliflower was able to walk over to the window and look out. Cauliflower was no show-off, so nobody knew about her linguistic abilities. She could speak the languages of many species of birds and was fluent in all the local dialects of Squirrel. She clicked to a squirrel in a tree she could see through her window, and they had this brief conversation.

"Hi, squirrel."

"Hi squirrel-not-squirrel. Mother of all squirrels. Not squirrel. All squirrel is I squirrel you squirrel, I squirrel.. Rolling in special dirt," clicked the squirrel.

"Rolling in special dirt to you and yours," clicked Cauliflower.

Stickle sat in the tree as well. He did not manifest himself in any way to Cauliflower, as he did not want to cause trouble. She did not know he was there. His newfound sobriety had made him a little more agile and adventurous, so, on impulse, he decided to climb a tree, the first time he had done so in one hundred and sixty years.

Had he fulfilled his mission? He thought that maybe he was close, and then again, maybe he was as far from accomplishing it as he ever had been. The squirrels were talking about heaven, which was beautiful, but was what they were saying accurate? He had no way of knowing because he had never been there. All he could do was provide hints.

Eggplant Charlie got most of his strength back, and since it had become clear that his wounds had not been inflicted by Cauliflower, he was finally allowed to see his wife. The co-op customers had been calling all day to demand her release, and the hospital administration had to explain that she was, indeed, free to go, but that she wouldn't leave without Eggplant Charlie, who was no longer exhibiting symptoms of Ardillian Paralysis Syndrome, and could leave the hospital the next day.

There were political repercussions concerning the video. There was talk of recalling the Sheriff in a special election, but he headed off that challenge by firing Tad Chen and Jubal Djumich, both of whom later found employment at the Home Depot on the state line. Redneck Davey liked to go there to tease them about their bright orange aprons and to ask where non-existent roofing supplies like thirteen-penny toe nails might be stored.

News of Cauliflower's exoneration did not spread as quickly or as extensively as the initial viral video of the incident that had unjustly tarnished her reputation. It didn't really matter. Fifteen minutes of fame—or notoriety—is mercifully short. The news did make it up to New York City, however, whereupon the *New York Times* art critic announced that the film was a classic now, on the order of the Kurosawa film *Rashomon*. The critic argued that the film had gone from being an exploration of the concept of deviance to an examination of power and its use and abuse in society. He still loved it. His appetite for crap had not diminished one iota.

Anyway, Eggplant Charlie and Cauliflower left together the next day. Mark Metacomet had managed to rescue the GMC from the lot to which it had been towed, and graciously drove them both back to the farm before taking off on foot for whatever Lilith had in store for him.

Home never looked so good to Eggplant Charlie, but he was obviously troubled by something.

"What's wrong?" asked Cauliflower.

"You know something weird? I died in the hospital. My heart stopped beating."

"They told me that. Did you go to heaven?"

"No. A ghost held me back. Thing is, I couldn't see where I was going, but I could see where I'd been."

"What do you mean?"

"I mean I could see a little of who I was before I was me. I couldn't see heaven, but I knew I'd been there."

"If you died and went to heaven, why did you come back?" asked Cauliflower.

"I thought I had unfinished business—something I'd started a long time ago and hadn't been able to finish."

"What was that?"

"Saving humanity. Making people quit hurting and killing other people."

"That doesn't sound like you. You don't like people very much."

"That's what scares me. I think I came down here for the wrong reason. I just wanted to finish a job, and I was supposed to do it because I loved everybody. All I've done in this life is grow vegetables. I'm failing at my mission," said Eggplant Charlie.

"Well, I didn't die at the hospital, but they gave me a lot of drugs, and I had to meditate real hard to keep them from messing up my system," said Cauliflower.

"I'm glad you're okay, hon."

"While I was meditating, my third eye opened, and I could see a lot of stuff, too."

"Like what?"

"We knew each other way back then. We've known each other for fifty thousand years."

"That doesn't surprise me, somehow," said Eggplant Charlie.

"Well, you're no worse than you ever were. You did great things then, and you're maybe doing things that aren't quite as great now, but you're the same person."

"I'm afraid I bit off more than I could chew. The world has changed a lot. I can't save humanity."

"You feed people good nutritious vegetables. You charge them a fair price. You don't like people much, but you're not mean to them."

"How can I re-enter heaven if I don't like people very much?"

"Do you hate people?"

"Not really. No."

"So you're not really *doing* anything right?"

"Right. I guess so."

"You are just *being*."

"Right."

"That's all you have to do. Just let yourself *be*."

Stickle would have to represent himself at Celestial Court for his parole hearing. Bones was nowhere to be found, and he probably wouldn't have been the best choice for a lawyer, anyway.

"Stephen Ray Stickle, you have petitioned the Court for relief. Will you explain yourself, sir?"

"Yes. I feel that I am ready to enter the kingdom, having fulfilled my mission to the best of my ability, and having broken my attachment to 'demon' alcohol."

"Do you really think that squirrels understand the concept of heaven?"

"Well, they can hint at it, which is all I was ever able to do."

"You're willing to leave every vestige of your former self behind? There is nothing that you absolutely must have with you now?"

"Nothing. I was born with nothing, and I died with nothing, and I aim to bring nothing with me if I am allowed to enter the Kingdom."

"You seem to have changed for the better, and your experience as a righteous ghost seems to have done wonderful things for your soul. We'll let you pass."

And a heavenly choir sang *Hannah Slumbers 'Neath the Sweet Gum Tree* as the angels danced.

THE END

About the Author

Walt Babich teaches English as a Second Language at the University of Delaware. He has previously worked as a construction worker, a bar musician, and an archaeological technician.